Las Vegas Haunted

Janice Oberding

Thunder Mountain Productions Press   Reno Nevada

Published by Thunder Mountain Productions Press
PO Box 19514
Reno, Nevada 89511

ISBN: 0-9721626-4-X

For Bonnie Harper and Roy Harper
My two favorite Las Vegans

TABLE OF CONTENTS

Acknowledgments

Writing is a solitary endeavor, but a book is seldom written without the help of others. Quiet time, time allocated for writing and little else, is a necessity. Thankfully I have a husband and family that understand. When necessary, my husband Bill is willing to jump in with the mop and the dinner dishes, as well as the camera and the notebook. My sons Billy and Fred never miss the opportunity to offer encouragement and advice, some needed, some not. I've also been blessed with two wonderful daughters-in-law, Peggy and Michelle. Although they are full time professionals, these two women that my sons chose so wisely, are so generous with their assistance.

I owe a tremendous debt of gratitude to my mom Bonnie Harper and "dad" Roy Harper. Without their insiders' knowledge of Las Vegas and their willingness to drive me all over Clark County and accompany me everywhere I wanted to go, this book could not have been written. My mother is a writer in her own right; her advice on the writing of this book is also acknowledged and appreciated.

Thanks to my fun loving nephew Dalvante Hursh who agreed to share his scary experience. Special thanks to my dear friends Tom and Lisa Butler whose friendship I treasure.

In addition I wish to acknowledge and thank Suzanne Turgeon of the Clark County Museum, John Hosier,

General Manager of Carluccios Tivoli Gardens Restaurant, Robert Allen of Haunted Vegas Tours, Tim Cridland, for the heads up on Hartland Mansion. David Emmett of Las Vegas Villa, Dixie Dooley, and Julie Brown of Escape the Magic Show.

Forward

Aah! Las Vegas, a city of neon, as bright and alive at 2:am as it is in the middle of the day. Visitors come to this oasis in the desert from all over the world. Many like it so well, they do not want to leave. So they go back home, sell their property and return as permanent residents.

There are also others that have been residing here in Las Vegas for a very long time; many believe they will remain throughout eternity. They are the ghosts Janice visits in the pages of this book. Some are famous, some not so famous. A few fit the truly infamous category. All are interesting.

One can easily understand why those of great talent and wealth might not want to give it all up entirely. Who knows? They might enjoy watching the throngs who gaze fondly at their likenesses and other memorabilia. Perhaps they find pleasure in playing host to our city's visitors.

Janice and I have visited the places that she writes about. To say she has had some interesting experiences is indeed an understatement. One particular incident occurred at the Old Logandale School in Logandale. Janice and I were walking down the hall when she suddenly jumped. "You're not going to believe this," she said. "But someone just tugged on my skirt. I looked at her floor length skirt. Was it possible she had actually tripped over her own skirt?

As if she were reading my mind, Janice said, "No Mama! I didn't trip over my skirt."

Later we were told that the little boy ghost likes pulling such pranks on those who visit the school museum.

Do ghosts exist? No one has proven absolutely that they do. No one has proven absolutely that they do not. Keep this in mind if you are walking alone on a dark street just outside of Las Vegas and happen upon a lonely figure that simply disappears as you approach. It has been said that," What happens in Las Vegas stays in Las Vegas."

Bonnie Harper
Las Vegas NV

Introduction

Las Vegas mayor, Oscar Goodman calls his city the most exciting city in the world. It is that, and more. There's glamour, excitement, sunshine (more sunny days here than there are in Florida,) opportunity, and a sense of being part of a city that is truly phenomenal (relatively new, Las Vegas is the only major city to come into being during the 20th century.) This one-of-a-kind city is Nevada's largest. And yet…the city was actually part of the Arizona Territory until Nevada's state boundary was rearranged in 1867. Nevada's gain to be sure!

Certainly there is a dark and quirky side to Sin City, there are problems; every major city has problems, so what? Nothing's perfect…not even Las Vegas. But it's close. The city has blasted and blown up most of its reminders of a not so distant past. It has renovated, and reinvented itself countless times since those nights when the Rat Pack slurped cocktails and swapped jokes at the Sands.

In the past few years Las Vegas has sprawled beyond even Bugsy's wildest dreams. All that remains of those long ago days when weary travelers stopped at the Las Vegas Ranch for water and refreshment is the replica of the Old Mormon Fort. A trickle of water snakes its way past shade trees and clumps of grass and rocks. Don't be fooled. Like many of Las Vegas' attractions, the creek is a replica; the area's ever growing demand for water long ago sucked the original creek dry.

One hundred years and still going strong....What happens in Las Vegas stays in Las Vegas. It's a great slogan, and it's especially apropos when one considers ghosts and hauntings.

Is Las Vegas haunted? Absolutely! There are ghosts here just as there are ghosts everywhere, some are famous, others are not; they are the restless spirits who've chosen, for whatever reasons to stay and stay and stay. And I can't say that I blame them. Why would a ghost hang out in a cemetery with the dazzle of Las Vegas beckoning? Why indeed!

Long Ago in the Meadows

Cemetery stories, they are always the same.
We walk among the headstones
in search of a familiar name.

Centuries before Bugsy, the Rat Pack, Elvis, and those who would help to transform this spot in the desert, the land was green, and watery, and alive with creatures long extinct.
Their end would come in a flash; the lushness of the region would perish slowly, in time, the verdant land would become a dry unforgiving desert.

Thousands of years ago the Anasazi lived along the Muddy and Virgin Rivers near present day Overton. A peaceful people, the first group is categorized as the Basketmakers for their utilitarian use of the baskets, they wove from yucca plants and willows. They hunted for deer, big horn sheep, lizards and rabbits using an atlatl (spear thrower.) The Basketmaker II was the next civilization to live in here.

Like the Basketmaker I, their cooking and storage implements were woven baskets. Instead of the atlatl, they hunted with the more effective bows and arrows, The Puebloans was the last ancient culture to live here. Unlike the Basketweavers, they used clay in the making of their utensils. An industrious people, they farmed crops such as corn, cotton and beans. Long before Comstock miners in the northern part of Nevada discovered silver, these people were mining turquoise and salt as valuable commodities.

And then, they would vanish, leaving more questions than answers. Remnants of their civilization, and its secrets, would lie hidden deep beneath the hard dry soil for centuries.

Seeking a route between their missions in Arizona and those in California, Spanish missionaries first entered present-day southern Nevada sometime around 1776. Fifty years later Antonio Armijo's party of traders was traveling along the Spanish Trail when the scout, Rafael Rivera decided to take a short cut. Whatever his reasons, he was rewarded with a breathtaking sight. Before him lush, verdant natural springs glittered in the scorching sun. Word quickly spread of the welcoming oasis with its cool relief from the hostile desert environment; soon others would find their way to the natural springs. This area would become known as "Las Vegas," which is Spanish for the meadows.

Explorer Jedidiah Smith, who traversed the area of Southern Nevada in 1826, was the first to make reference to the salt caves and other relics of a past civilization located in the region. The Lost City Museum displays a replica of the following words Smith wrote to William

Clark the Superintendent of Indian Affairs, on July 12, 1827.

The Paiutes have a number of marble pipes, one of which I obtained and sent to you. Although it has been broken since I have had it in my possession; they told me there was a quantity of the same material south of their country. I also obtained a knife of flint, which I send you, but it has likewise been broken by accident.

This early discovery by Jedidiah Smith went almost unnoticed and aroused little curiosity. Captain John C. Fremont would change that with his 1845 expedition of the area.

Of what would later become Las Vegas, Fremont wrote, "...we encamped in the midst of another very large basin, at a camping ground called Las Vegas -- a term which the Spaniards use to signify fertile or marshy plains, in contradistinction to llanos, which they apply to dry and sterile plains. Two narrow streams of clear water, four or five feet deep, gush suddenly with a quick current, from two singularly large springs; these, and other waters of the basin, pass out in a gap to the eastward. The taste of the water is good, but rather too warm to be agreeable; the temperature being 71 in the one and 73 in the other. They, however, afford a delightful bathing place."

The way would further be paved for emigrants and merchants to this area when in 1846 Congress printed 20,000 copies of his report on the expedition and Charles Preuss' map of the area.

Lost City

In 1924 two brothers Fay and John Perkins were prospecting for gold in a remote area of the Southern Nevada desert when they happened upon remnants of a lost civilization. The men dutifully notified Nevada Governor James Scrugham of their find; Scrugham, a former state engineer, was quick to realize the importance of the discovery and sought help from outside sources in the excavation and study of the area. Soon worldwide attention would be focused on Nevada and its Lost City.

Estimates put the site at 7000 years old. After a closer examination the Lost City was believed to date from 1500 to 2000 BC. The first excavations yielded a treasure trove for archaeologists: buried houses (pueblos,) clothing, tools household items and skeletons buried in the floors or walls of the communal houses.

Nearly six miles square, the site had now become known as Pueblo Grande de Nevada; it stirred the imagination and intrigued scientists, and scholars who came to the desert to see the ancient ruins for themselves. They went about their work, relentlessly salvaging, tagging and categorizing their finds. But time was not on the side of those who tirelessly sifted through the ruins. Plans for a project that would dam part of the Colorado River, and redirect its flow were already in the works.

With the completion of Hoover Dam (Boulder Dam) the Colorado River was redirected and the manmade Lake Mead was formed. As the waters of the lake began to swell early Nevada towns like St.Thomas were lost forever. So too was the ancient Pueblo Grande, the Lost City. Even so, there are still miles of ruins along the Moapa Valley yet to be excavated and studied.

Lost City Museum

The fascinating history of the Lost City Pueblo Grande de Nevada is preserved at the Lost City Museum in Overton, which owns one of the most complete collections of the early Pueblo Indians of the Southwest. Starting with the Desert Culture that lived here 10,000 years ago and continuing on through the Ancient Basketmaker I, II and III cultures, the display features many artifacts and treasures recovered from the Pueblo Grande before it was forever submerged beneath the waters of Lake Mead.

Some claim the ghosts of those who lived here long ago haunt the museum and the grounds surrounding it. The sound of singing and laughter has been reportedly heard on the grounds near the replica adobe pueblos.

Replica pueblos where strange noise has been reported

Kiel Ranch Front Porch   Library of Congress

Kiel Ranch Mystery

Time has passed. The city has grown and slowly encroached upon what was once one of the largest ranches in the area. All that remains of the old Kiel Ranch is a large lot surrounded by a padlocked chain link fence. Locked behind the fence are thick patches of drought resistant weeds, scattered debris and the burned out replica of a ranch house. Las Vegas area's first mystery was played out here on a long ago July morning. Perhaps no one will ever know the truth of that day, except for the lonely ghosts who roam this area.

It was July 1884. The day was like any other summer day in this region; the heat grew more intense as the sun rose higher in the sky. Her chores done, Mrs. Helen Stewart and her children took refuge on their shady front porch. Fanning herself absently, she looked up and saw a horse and rider hurrying toward her. Dust flew in all directions as the man spurred the horse on. What, she wondered, could be the reason for such haste, especially on a day like this.

A moment later her question would be answered; the horse came to a stop in front of the porch and the rider quickly slid from the saddle. Silently he handed her a neatly folded piece of paper, remounted and turned toward the Kiel Ranch. She unfolded the paper and stared at it in disbelief.

Mrs. Stewart your husband is here dead. Come and take him away.

She read the cruel words several more times before crumpling the paper. Questions raced through her mind, but for now she would do what had to be done. Leaving her children in the care of a kitchen helper, she hitched up her wagon and headed for the Kiel Ranch with two ranch hands.

Mr. Kiel was waiting for her. He touched his hat ever so briefly, and then grimly pointed to a still form that lay on the ground covered by a heavy woolen blanket. It was too hot for blankets. She stooped and pulled a corner of the blanket back. The dead man was indeed her husband; his

fatal injuries were evident. Helen Stewart touched the familiar face, and blinking back tears, she stood.

"How did this happen, Mr. Kiel?"

"Self-defense. So says Schuyler Henry and Hank Parrish."

He stared at her coldly. "I was not here when the shooting started. But I am told that your husband came here gun drawn and looking for a fight. This," he nodded toward the corpse, "is the result."

"I see."

But she didn't. None of this made any sense, no sense at all. With four children and another one on the way, Mrs. Stewart wanted only the safety of her own home. She'd never liked or trusted the elder Mr. Kiel, somehow he was involved, and she knew it. She would sort everything out later, and then she would contact the sheriff. Ranch hands carefully loaded Archibald Stewart's lifeless body onto the wagon and his widow headed back toward their ranch.

A month later a grand jury was convened in Pioche. Mrs. Stewart was bitterly disappointed with their verdict of self-defense. She would go on to successfully raise her children, become a well-respected businesswoman and the first woman to serve on a jury in the city of Las Vegas, but she would never forget.

Those who had lain in wait to murder Archibald Stewart were free to go on with their lives. But fate would eventually catch up with them.

Hank Parrish would hang in Ely a few years later for the cold-blooded murder of yet another man.

October 11, 1900. Fierce winds swept across the valley with the promise of fall and its respite, however brief, from the heat that shortened men's tempers and shriveled crops still on the vine. In a coincidence that boggles the mind and seems to flout the laws of probability, Archibald Stewart's son Hiram and his foreman went to the Kiel Ranch to visit and do business with neighbors Edwin and William Kiel, the sons of Conrad Kiel.

When no one answered their knock, they waited a few minutes then stepped inside the house. Something wasn't right here; it was too quiet. They glanced toward the kitchen and discovered Edwin's lifeless body sprawled across the floor; a gunshot wound to the head had cut short his stay on this earth.

Calling to William, the men cautiously backed out the door and started looking for the other Kiel brother. Moments later they found him nearly submerged in the irrigation ditch some yards from the house. William's injuries appeared to be more substantial than those of his brother, a shotgun wound in the left arm, a second in the chest and a third bullet lodged near his left eye.

A coroner's jury later determined that Edwin had killed William in a fit of rage; filled with remorse at what he done, he'd turned the gun on himself. There were whispers around the valley and many people wondered if Hiram Stewart hadn't taken revenge on the Kiel brothers for his father's untimely death. Just as that of Archibald Stewart had been sixteen years earlier, the Kiels' deaths would remain shrouded in mystery.

Edwin and William were buried in wooden coffins beside their father in the family cemetery on the Kiel Ranch; the truth of their deaths seemed destined to be just one more mystery. Then, in 1975 came an opportunity to discover some answers in the case of the three deaths. The body of Archibald Stewart was to be exhumed at the site of the old Las Vegas Ranch and the city of North Las Vegas began to expand.

In a world whose resources are continually being depleted, progress must sometimes make way for the living at the expense of the dead; the cemetery would be excavated and the bodies removed. Forensic experts at the University of Nevada Las Vegas Anthropology Department set to work and soon discovered that Archibald Stewart had been felled by two different weapons. This bears out statements that were made by some who had seen his body shortly before burial. In the case Kiel Brothers Edwin was vindicated. Another interesting findings was the fact that the angle of William 's wounds indicated there might have been more than one killer at the Kiel Ranch.

What was the reason behind the cold blooded killing of the Kiel Brothers? Who had murdered them? Could their killings have been in retaliation for that of Archibald Stewart?

Some of those who played near the old Kiel Ranch when there were empty lots all around, have told of strange noises and fleeting sights caught in an instant out of the corner of an eye. A ghostly Archibald Stewart caught in the final moments of his life? The spirits of the Kiel Brothers as they face their ghostly assailants? All three men are said to haunt the old Kiel Ranch area. A ghostly man has been seen running across the area where the old ranch house once stood, and there have also been reports of strange noises in the area.

It is well known among ghost researchers that a violent, unexpected death may give rise to paranormal activity. This is the place of three violent and unexpected deaths. The killers of the Kiel Brothers escaped justice, and if Archibald Stewart was killed, not in self-defense, but in cold blood, his killers also managed to escape the law. Could it be then that the ghosts of Kiel Ranch want merely to right old wrongs?

Stewart Ranch House

Old Las Vegas Mormon Fort

A replica of the old Mormon Fort is located on North Las Vegas Boulevard at Washington Avenue. It was on this spot that the city of Las Vegas began. Among the interesting items at the old fort are the first flag that flew over Las Vegas, farming and household implements and photos of Helen and Archibald Stewart. (The adobe wall in the photo above is all that remains of the old Mormon Fort.)

William Bringhurst, and other Mormon missionaries, came here from Utah in 1855 to settle the region. They built a fort that was little more than an adobe walled enclosure. Within the enclosure they planted crops and used water from the creek and the nearby springs for their irrigation.

Most of the crops flourished. But the blistering desert heat proved too much for the settlers who abandoned the site after only two years. In 1865 Octavius D. Gass purchased the land and proceeded to build the large Las Vegas Ranch. Sixteen years later he lost the property to Archibald Stewart when he defaulted on a loan.

The Stewart family owned the ranch for many years until in 1902 Helen Steward, with uncanny foresight, sold the land and the water rights to the San Pedro, Los Angeles and Salt Lake Railroad. Mrs. Helen Steward would continue to live in the city and to play an important part in early day Las Vegas. Today she is known as the First Lady of Las Vegas.

At least one ghost is said to walk the grounds of the old ranch late at night. Described as gaunt, the phantom is usually spotted near the site of the old ranch house, or at the replica of the pioneer garden. Perhaps the ghostly Archibald Stewart, who was murdered so long ago, still oversees his ranch.

Old adobe at Mormon Fort circa 1905   Old Mormon Fort

GANGSTERS

Don't worry. We only kill each other…..Bugsy Siegel

My Man Bugsy Blues

Generally credited as being the father of modern Las Vegas, Bugsy Siegel is also the city's most famous ghost. He probably would have liked all the attention.

Benjamin Siegel was born to immigrant parents in a poor New York neighborhood on February 20, 1906. From an early age he was determined to have it all. As a teenager he met Meyer Lansky and together they formed a group of young street thugs who thought nothing of robbing, maiming, and even killing, anyone who stood in their way.

When Meyer Lansky sent him to Los Angeles in the early 1930's to straighten out personnel problems, Bugsy discovered that he liked Hollywood, especially the movie star ambiance. So he rented a large home in nearby Beverly Hills and moved his wife and children in. Ever the ladies' man, he didn't let a little thing like a family stand in the way of his romantic pursuits with several well known stars of the day. Occasionally he would head for a little rest and relaxation in the desert gambling town of Las Vegas, some 100 miles east.

Gambling had only been legalized in Nevada a few years; watching people happily engaged in the pursuit of winning, Siegel was intrigued with how much of their money they were willing to risk at the tables, the roulette wheels and the slots. He may have only had an 8th grade education, but Bugsy was smart enough to figure the odds.

There was a tremendous amount of money to be made here in Las Vegas. And it was legal. The suckers couldn't wait to hand over their cash. Gambling, they said. But Bugsy knew better. He was nobody's fool; the odds are always in the house's favor. Sooner or later, the house wins..Always!

Las Vegas had seen its shot at fame come and go with the Boulder Dam Project. Nearly 40 years old and straggling behind Reno as gambling's fun spot, the city needed to head in a new direction. Bugsy Siegel would see that it did. He'd come to take care of Lansky's horserace betting operation

While Siegel oversaw the interests of Meyer Lansky, restaurateur, publisher and gambler Billy Wilkerson kept busy watching his dream take shape in the form of a highbrow gambling establishment. He was ready to show these cowboys a thing or two about class. Black tie, evening attire, there would be no rowdy, casually attired, kick-ass cowboys in his place; unless they were sweeping the floors, or washing the dishes. Even then, they would be required to exchange the boots and the blue jeans for high-class uniforms.

Wilkerson easily schmoozed with the stars in Beverly Hills and by God he could schmooze with them here in the desert. All he had to do was get them here. In time, they would come.

Bugsy admired class. He liked what he saw and suddenly wanted what Wilkerson had. And in true Bugsy fashion, he shoved Wilkerson outta his dream and into an agreement. A legal document was drawn up. Ever the gambler, Wilkerson figured the odds and gladly signed on the dotted line; giving away his dream beat taking up permanent residence in a six-foot plot of the Southern Nevada desert. No dreams there.

The Flamingo Hotel was on its way to becoming a reality and for the time being Benjamin "Bugsy" Siegel was in charge. In Vegas years, the clock was ticking.....

Not everyone agreed with Bugsy about the Flamingo. On August 1, 1946 The Las Vegas Tribune carried a front page editorial criticizing him for having the audacity to use scarce material in the building of a casino. According to the editorial, this material could be put to better use by building homes for returning war veterans. Especially since the Civilian Production Administration (CPA) was organized for the purpose of building homes rather than commercial establishments. None of this mattered; Whether or not he'd used bribery as a means of securing them, Bugsy had obtained his building permits from the Civilian Production Administration and construction continued.

Bugsy held tight to his bosses' purse strings; the war had just ended and materials were difficult to come by. Anything that could be obtained was generally overpriced, and then there were the delays and the thefts. One rumor involves workers stealing material in the evening only to redeliver and recharge for it the next day. Bugsy, who would eventually pay with his life for the cost overruns, was none the wiser. He might have been an excellent gangster, but Siegel was no businessman. Worse he liked to spend money, especially on horses, dining, and squiring beautiful women.

After patiently waiting for him to stop his philandering, Bugsy's wife finally decided enough was enough and filed for divorce in Reno. This left Bugsy more time to pursue the new woman in his life; Virginia Hill was beautiful and vivacious and liked to spend money. It didn't matter whose money she spent.

It's a widely held belief that Virginia and Bugsy were stealing from his bosses in order to finance their lavish lifestyle, and this is the real reason that Bugsy was killed. The thefts might not have been so bad, had the Flamingo made money early on. But luck was against Bugsy on opening night December 1946.

Finally, at a cost of over five million dollars the Flamingo was open. It was wintertime in Las Vegas. A freak storm had hit the West Coast in full force. As heavy wind driven rain washed across the valley, Jimmy Durante, Rose Marie and other top name entertainers attempted to please the sparse crowd of gamblers who'd braved the elements to come out and see what the Flamingo was all about.

Notably absent was the western cowpoke look of the other Las Vegas establishments. The décor was modern up to the minute swank; class as interpreted by Benjamin Siegel. No bolo ties, boots or plaid shirts. Bugsy and staff were attired in formal wear. This probably seemed pretentious to those who were accustomed to the El Rancho Vegas and its heavy western theme. No one dared voice such an opinion as Bugsy greeted his guests warmly.

The hotel was still not complete, so as they grew weary of gambling, the customers had little choice but to leave the premises, taking their money with them. Three hundred miles away in Los Angeles would be patrons were kept away because the raging winter storm had grounded all planes. This was not at all what Bugsy had envisioned. Eventually he would be proven right; the Flamingo would become a huge money making success. Unfortunately Bugsy wouldn't be around to see it. On this night his bosses were furious with him. They'd squandered enough money in the Nevada desert. Now Siegel was on a crash course with destiny. No one could save him, not even his childhood friend Meyer Lansky.

The end came for Bugsy on June 20, 1947. He never saw it coming. In Las Vegas he'd prepared for violence by surrounding himself with a retinue of bodyguards. His penthouse at the Flamingo was locked behind a steel reinforced door, the windows were bullet proof, and in the closet was a special secret ladder escape that would take him to an awaiting getaway car in the garage tunnel that could lead him to safety in the eventuality...

810 Linden Street, Virginia Hill's rented Beverly Hills home. Virginia was in Europe. Later, opinions would differ as to whether she had been out of town by accident, luck or design. The heat hung in the air, undisturbed by so much as a wisp of a breeze. Darkness had fallen, but it would be hours before the night cooled off.

Bugsy and his friend returned from their early dinner and settled onto the sofa. He casually glanced at his newspaper and switched on a reading lamp. When silence eventually fell between them he would read the paper. Their conversation was idle, old friend chitchat, punctuated by laughter.

The killers silently crept up the long driveway to the mansion. Theirs was a job that required stealth and cunning. The target was in full view, relaxed and unaware of what fate had decreed. They took aim...Three shots rang out in quick succession...Bugsy was no more. A shattered bloody corpse slumped on the colorful chintz sofa.

It would not be the end of the Flamingo, only a change of management. Within hours of his death things were back to normal at his beloved Flamingo. Dead or not, Bugsy's dream would go on. While five mourners gathered to see him off to his final resting place, gamblers eagerly tossed their money into the Flamingo's coffers.

And he is remembered still. His vision paved the way for Southern Nevada's hotel/casino industry and in celebration of their 50th anniversary, the Flamingo remembered him by putting his likeness on their five-dollar chips.

Bugsy was killed in Beverly Hills but his apparition was reportedly spotted numerous times in his penthouse suite at the Flamingo before the building was razed in 1996. Since that time, the ghostly gangster has usually been spotted at the wedding chapel or in the rose garden near the plaque that bears his likeness and an inscription.

Ghosts are not necessarily consigned to the places of their death. If they are of free will and able to go to the spots they enjoyed in life, it stands to reason that Bugsy would seek out the Flamingo.

Some items pertaining to Bugsy are on display at the Nevada Historical Society located in Lorenzi Park. These items include photos of the Flamingo, the door to his penthouse, a chandelier from the penthouse, an agreement signed between him and Billy Wilkerson and a scissors set. Bugsy would be pleased to know that there's not a Bugsy in the bunch, everything is labeled as having belonged to Benjamin Siegel.

Chandelier that lit Bugsy's world in his Flamingo Penthouse

Bonnie and Clyde car   Bill Oberding

Bonnie and Clyde; No Ghosts Here

It is just as well that bank robbers/killers Bonnie Parker and Clyde Barrow never made it to Las Vegas. The cold-blooded twosome was dispatched from this world in a merciless hail of bullets near Sailes, Bienville Parish, Louisiana in the early morning hours of May 23, 1934.

After the public's insatiable curiosity was satisfied with several photos of the pair dead as dead could be, both were buried in Dallas Texas. Yes, it was the end for Bonnie and Clyde, but unlike Bonnie predicted in her poem, they do not repose side by side.

41

The car that took the lawless pair on their ride into eternity can be seen at the Primm Fashion Mall, as can the conveyance of Dutch Shultz. When asked if there are any reports of the car being haunted, employees are quick to say, "No."

However, some of those who have worked on the car say that they've seen people sitting in the infamous auto. Others claim to have experienced feelings of foreboding and terror when they stood near the car. Given the extent of violence, this isn't surprising.

Now that the car can only be viewed behind glass some of the strange feelings may subside. Maybe!

Tony, The Ant Spilotro

A través de la puerta
vienen los muertos.

Like Bugsy Siegel before him, Tony Spilotro was a mobster. And like Bugsy, when it was time for Spilotro to exit the Las Vegas scene, he was killed elsewhere.

That's where the similarities end. Bugsy was handsome and suave; Spilotro was anything but. Siegel has reportedly come back to his beloved Las Vegas. If he has, the ghostly Spilotro is keeping a low profile. Then again, perhaps his apparition still wanders through that Indiana cornfield trying to figure out how he went wrong.

The Las Vegas of the 1970's was very different from the Las Vegas of today. Spilotro had the juice. And was making piles of money. Then he went and pissed the wrong people off.

Strange as it seems, some Las Vegans that worked in the service industry remember him as being kindhearted. Said a waitress, who waited on him several times at a hotel/casino that has long since been imploded,

"He was always nice to me...always left me a good toke. When he was with a group of people who had finished their meal, he would ask them, 'What about the girl? Did you leave her a tip?' If they didn't answer him, he'd asked me, 'Honey did they get you?'

I knew who he was. Everyone did. And I knew who they were. So I just smiled and said, 'Yes sir. '

Another person, who wasn't impressed with Spilotro's generosity laughed, "Obviously good tokes don't mean jack when it comes to getting whacked in a cornfield. "

Obviously not!

STARS

I cry all the way to the bank…Liberace

Stars are Different...

Ghostly famous people are spotted more often than ordinary people. Living or dead, the stars will always be with us. Those who achieved fame and glory in life may have a difficult time giving it all up. Denial may set in and the rationale could be I'm a star, I can't be dead.

Even after the grim reaper has tapped them on the shoulder and said, "come along quietly," many famous folks might decide to stay around simply because they can't bear to part with all their worldly possessions. It must be difficult to see others enjoying the fruits of one's labors. Especially if those others include heirs one never knew, managers, hangers on and the IRS.

Perhaps it is a misplaced sense of loyalty that keeps the ghostly stars with us. I owe it to my fans. What will they think of me now that I'm dead?

Of course there is also the fact that we, as human beings, usually see what we want to see. Surely it's less thrilling to be haunted by an average garden-variety ghost when one can just as easily be haunted by a star. After all, stars are different.

Whatever the reasons ghostly stars are here to stay...

Redd Foxx Strut

John Ellroy Sanford, yes that was his real name, came to Las Vegas at a time when African-Americans were not even welcome to stay in the high class hotel/casinos. Entertainers like Lena Horne and Sammy Davis Jr. were drawing customers to the gaming establishments, yet they were consigned to the Westside of town. In time, Sammy Davis Jr., Frank Sinatra and others would help to right this terrible wrong...

But Sanford didn't give up so easily. He intended on making it big in showbiz. In the meantime, he lived by his wry wit. Some called his routine vulgar; others laughed their asses off, and loved every minute of it. Sanford's talent propelled him to the top.

When he arrived, it was as Redd Foxx. Foxx quickly became the mainstay of casinos eager to entertain their guests. As a testament to his star status, he built a home, complete with swimming pool, on Eastern Avenue. There he settled in to live the good life. As time passed his fame continued to rise.

Television execs were watching. Wouldn't this Redd Foxx be great? If we could clean up his act...There were no foul mouthed, four letter words permitted on television at that time. The execs had spoken, and it was done. Foxx slid into the role of the cotton topped Fred Sanford as easy as a showgirl slaps on her eyelashes. Audiences adored him, but there were problems with the shows' executives. Finally

Foxx and the show parted company. He was on top of his game, Vegas time was flying, and the IRS wanted their piece of the big money pie. It seemed that Redd owed them a bundle.

In 1991 Foxx went to work on The Royal Family a new weekly show that co-starred his old friend Della Reese. For a time it looked as if things had finally turned around for the comedian. Then, on October 11, 1991 one month after the first episode aired, Redd Foxx toppled over on the set, dead of a massive heart attack. Dead or alive, one's taxes must be paid.

Now the IRS was set to collect; the Foxx home was put up for sale. It sold quickly, and the new owner moved in. Almost immediately strange things began to happen. First it was the cold unexplained breezes. No obvious reasons for the drafts could be found. Then the doors and windows began to open and close on their own. Believing that the home was haunted, the new owner decided to sell the home and move out.

Red Foxx pool   Bill Oberding

The home was converted for commercial use and a business moved in. No sooner did they open their doors than employees began seeing the apparition of Redd Foxx . Occasionally he would appear in the room that had once been his bedroom. Other times he was spotted walking down the hallway or outdoors by the swimming pool. Items were moved about and the doors continued to open and close of their own volition. Sensing that he meant only to stay in residence, no one was frightened of the ghostly comedian. Eventually the business moved out and another moved in. Once in a while voices of unseen people laughing and talking can still be heard in the back of the building.

Redd Foxx living room during renovation   Bill Oberding

Rat Pack Rondelet

During the 1950's and the 1960's the Rat Pack were regulars at the Sands in Las Vegas. The pack made up of Sammy Davis Jr., Peter Lawford, Joey Bishop, Dean Martin, and of course Frank Sinatra, who owned a small percentage of the Sands, kept the casino's patrons happy and entertained with their songs, and good-natured repartee.

In 1960 the rat pack went to work on a new film in Las Vegas. Ocean's 11 is the story of a group of men who carry out a daring plan to rip off five Las Vegas casinos on New Years Eve: the Sands, the Desert Inn, Riviera, the Sahara and the Flamingo. It's a small world, especially in Las Vegas. Those making cameo appearances in the film were Red Skelton and George Raft, who happened to be an actor pal of Bugsy Siegel. The movie was well received; Las Vegas and the rat pack were now more popular than ever.

That same year John F. Kennedy defeated Richard M. Nixon and was elected to the presidency. Kennedy was in the White House and members of the rat pack suddenly found themselves with political connections; Peter Lawford was after all, the brother in law of the President of the United States. This was a more innocent time. It would be decades before the public became aware of Kennedy's womanizing and his supposed affairs with Marilyn Monroe and Judith Exner, a paramour of mobster Sam Giancana. The rat pack had connections, convoluted or not.

Giancana would figure prominently in the Nevada Gaming Control Boards' license revocation of Frank Sinatra's gaming license. Listed in the board's black book of those undesirables barred entrance to Nevada gaming establishments, Giancana visited Sinatra's Cal-Neva Lodge in the summer of 1963. That visit was well documented; it eventually cost Sinatra not only the Cal-Neva Lodge but also his percentage of ownership in the Sands. Las Vegas loved Sinatra. Mayor Hank Thornley presented a Proclamation of Appreciation to him in 1970 and in 1981 his gaming license was reinstated; it probably didn't hurt that one of his character witnesses was President Ronald Reagan.

Frank Sinatra and the Rat Pack are long gone. For that matter, so is the Las Vegas they once knew. Still, one can't help but wonder if the group doesn't occasionally sally forth and hold court in some little out of the way joint known only to them....

Elvis, You Can't Be Dead

Las Vegas adores Elvis. Anyone that doubts this only needs to look around; this is a city of Elvis impersonators. In the showrooms, laundromats, supermarkets and wedding chapels, Elvis look-a-likes are everywhere. It wasn't always so...

When he first appeared here at the New Frontier in 1956, Elvis wasn't the big hit he hoped to be. His style hadn't yet caught on. Blue suede shoes and waterfall hair might have appealed to teenagers, but it wasn't enough to really grab the more sophisticated showroom going crowd by their pocketbooks. So he honed his style in films like Blue Hawaii and Viva Las Vegas. One day he would be draw them.

In 1967 he and his girlfriend, Priscilla came to town like thousands of others and got married. Fans adored the stylish Priscilla with her heavily teased bouffant hairdo, and Queen-of the-Nile eye makeup. What they really loved however, were the changes in Elvis.

More than a decade had passed since he'd swiveled onto the Ed Sullivan Show. He was older and richer, had several movies to his credit, and seemed to be in the process of changing his look even further. In addition to the waterfall hair, he now sported dark luxurious sideburns.

With the 1970's came the plump Elvis cavorting on stage in a sequined jumpsuit and cape. Many of the teenage girls who'd swooned over his first film, *Love Me Tender*, were now middle-aged matrons. And they remembered. He sang for them and to them, swabbed himself with colorful scarves and then handed out the sweat drenched souvenirs to those lucky, or unlucky, enough to be sitting in the front rows. Audiences loved him. Hotel/Casinos clamored to put his name on their marquees; he could command top dollar for his appearances. Once again Elvis was back on top.

He had achieved it all; his abuse of prescription drugs and overeating continued. Then in August 1977 Elvis' world came crashing down around him. He was the king, he was 42 years old, and he was dead. All the king's medics, and all the king's money, couldn't breathe life back into the cold form on the floor of the master bathroom at Graceland.

Elvis couldn't be dead! James Dean be damned, stars aren't supposed to die. Came the hoax theory. Elvis wanted to shirk his fame and live the good life wandering the globe in happy anonymity. He was spotted everywhere, from Bangkok to Bakersfield.

One way or the other, the king must be kept alive if only in our hearts; for that it would take his fans undying devotion. It would take the hopes and dreams of those who wanted to be like him, sing like him, speak like him, and most of all be adored like him. While he had lived, his look was good for little more than a party joke, a Halloween costume. Now that he was gone Las Vegas latched onto the king in earnest.

From all across the country, Elvis impersonators descended on the city, some came in shades and outlandish wigs, others in white stretch jumpsuits sparkling with dime store spangles. All wanting their share of the glory that had been his. Some grew weary and went home. Others stuck it out, knowing as long as the Elvis image sold, there would be work.

The ghostly Elvis wasn't having any of it. He might have died in Memphis but he promptly returned to Las Vegas.

At least one person saw his apparition at the fabulous Hartland Mansion, located at the corner of Charleston and 6th Streets. Elvis was rumored to have stayed at the Hartland from time to time, while performing at the International Hotel.

Just as he'd been spotted in points across the globe, the ghost of Elvis began turning up in the backstage areas of some of local showrooms, particularly that of Hilton Hotel.

The apparition was Elvis the elder, plump and attired in the trademark jumpsuit. He handed out sweat stained scarves and vanished in the night; other times, he stood silently in the wings a moment and then he was gone...

Says one witness, "Call me crazy if you like. But I saw the ghost of Elvis, big as you please. I was working the graveyard shift at the time. I was polishing the floor about three in the morning when something just made me look up. That's when I saw him coming across the hall. At first I thought it was one of the impersonators...and then he just disappeared right there in front of me..."

One of the most famous people to have seen the apparition of Elvis is singer and Las Vegan, Wayne Newton. In his 1989 autobiography *Once Before I Go,* Newton tells of seeing the ghostly Elvis sitting in the balcony during one of his performances.

Some researchers of the paranormal believe that excessive grief or admiration can keep a spirit from making the necessary transition after death; like an anchor or a chain these strong emotions hold the spirit earthbound. Given the adulation he has received since his untimely death it wouldn't be too surprising then for Elvis to stay on.

Elvis may have left the building ladies and gentlemen, but apparently he hasn't left Las Vegas.

Sin City Séance: Summoning Elvis

Another anniversary of Elvis' death and storm clouds gathered over Las Vegas. Rain was in the forecast, hopefully enough would fall to dampen the soil and quench the thirst of area desert plants. No doubt the group that gathered in a local casino showroom on this dreary afternoon were hoping for something a bit more phenomenal, something unusual if you please.

Would the spirit of Elvis grace them with his presence, if only for a millisecond or two? Would a pair of blue suede shows suddenly materialize and tap out time with old Elvis tunes that played softly in the background? All eyes were on medium illusionist Dixie Dooley as he took to the stage and began the séance that would summon the dearly departed Elvis.

"Elvis! We know how much you love Las Vegas. You performed across the street. Are you here with us now?"

Silence!

Some of those in the audience squirmed in their seats nervously. Surely Elvis would deign to give some sort of sign to those so loyal to his memory.

"Elvis! If you're here with us will you please give us a sign."

At that moment thunder roared across the sky; rain began to pelt the roof.

"It's a sign!" Someone exclaimed.

"Maybe so," Dixie cautioned.

Rain continued to drench the building and the roof started to leak. It was turning out to be a wet and unusual day in the desert after all. The séance was concluded. Coincidence or not, had Elvis given a sign?

Tupac Shakur; Say It Ain't So

He takes my hand.

Don't you understand?

We are ghosts, you and I.

Tupac Shakur died on Friday the 13th. A drive by shooting; the deafening sound of gunfire and bullets shattering the tinted glass windows of the BMW. Five found their mark, cutting short a promising career and critically injuring the world famous actor, rapper.

Shakur was tough; he lingered six days before giving in to the inevitable. Distraught fans stormed the hospital and the coroner's office wanting a glimpse, just a glimpse of their idol in death. Nothing doing! Shakur's family ordered the twenty-five year old's remains be cremated ASAP.

What went wrong? Tupac Shakur was known to wear a bulletproof vest, but on the night of September 7th he'd decided against the added protection. It was just too hot.

Tupak and thousands of other fight fans had come to town for a championship boxing match between Mike Tyson and Bruce Seldon. The fight lasted only 103 seconds. Just enough time for Tyson to knock his opponent to the mat twice. A TKO.

As crowds poured from the MGM Grand a skirmish broke out at the hotel's entrance. Tupac jumped in. Then he and a friend whisked away in a black BMW. After a quick change of clothes, they were off again and headed toward a private party.

Along the way fate caught up with the handsome Shakur. At the corners of Koval and Flamingo Streets a white Cadillac pulled up alongside the BMW. Tupac didn't have time to react before the Cadillac's occupants opened fire.

It's difficult for fans to let go. Like Elvis before him, Tupac Shakur is rumored to still be living somewhere under an assumed name, with a complete new identity. As evidence, some point to the rap star's lyrics and to the fact that he predicted his own death. However, a published autopsy photo would seem to prove that Shakur is no longer of this world. Or is he?

At least one person claims to have seen the ghostly Tupac at the corner where he was fatally wounded.

"I drive down Koval on my way home from work every night. The first time I saw him I thought, that couldn't be, my imagination must be playing tricks on me...Then I saw him another time. Now I'm not so sure.

Tupac Shakur has also been spotted at a Las Vegas mansion. Nouveau California style, with lots of stucco and adobe tile, the million dollars plus home is surrounded by palm trees, pine trees, hedges and a stone fence. After dark, it's said, the ghostly rapper appears on the balcony and stares somberly into the distance.

Liberace and stewardess circa 1955

Liberace

Mr. Showmanship! Liberace was a handsome curly haired kid when he met Maxine Lewis, the woman who would help to make him a star. In 1944 Lewis, the entertainment director of the Last Frontier signed a contract with the pianist guaranteeing him $750.00 per week.

Watching his first performance Lewis was impressed. Liberace held his audience enthralled; he would certainly be a big star. The crowd's enthusiasm and acceptance portended nothing short of fame. An astute businesswoman, she upped his salary to $1500.00 after that first performance. It would not be the last salary increase for Liberace. By 1972 he was commanding $300,000 a year at the Hilton Hotel.

Liberace died in 1987 at his home in Palm Springs California. He was 67 years old. Charismatic and talented, his fans came from all walks of life, and from all over the world. Nowhere did he have more fans than in Las Vegas. There are still many people in town that remember his kindness and his culinary skills.

Of Liberace, one person who attended some of his dinner parties says, "Yes there was Gladys (the cook) but he was also a wonderful cook. He never seemed happier than when he was preparing a special meal for his friends. His personality was completely different than his stage persona."

Las Vegas will not forget Mr. Showmanship anytime soon. Apparently this is the way he wants it. And could be the reason he still haunts some of his favorite Sin City places.

There are No Ghosts on Debbie Reynolds Drive

Unless you count the ghosts of marriages past.

When Eddie Fisher dumped Debbie Reynolds for her good friend Liz Taylor he headed off to Las Vegas for his six weeks residency and quickie Nevada divorce. The plan was the two lovebirds would be wed soon as his wife was shed.

While Mr. Fisher and Ms. Taylor awaited their nuptial bliss, he appeared as the headliner at the Tropicana, and she sometimes sat near the stage swooning. Oh so romantic.

Too bad their marriage was as ill fated as his and the discarded Debbie's had been. Ah, but that was a long time ago... all is probably forgiven and forgotten...

But fate has a way of evening the score. Of the three, Debbie Reynolds is the only one who still performs regularly, and the only one that has a Las Vegas street named for her. Bravo Debbie!

Dixie Dooley; Makin Magic

Master magician Dixie Dooley's must see show *Escape the Magic Show* can be seen in Le Bistro at the Riviera. Sharing the stage with Dixie, and adding some pizzazz, are two talented and very lovely young women, Shedini (Escape Artist of the Year) and Julie Brown. Also on board is Kidd Famous who livens things up with his rap repertoire. But it is Dooley's personality and sense of humor, that shine through out this show. Yes! Dixie Dooley is his real name. The soft-spoken escape artist came to Las Vegas with the dream of performing Houdini escapes. In that he has succeeded. Extremely knowledgeable on Houdini, Dixie now wants to do some of his own things. No doubt he will succeed. Having participated in his Liberace séance, I was impressed with his no nonsense approach. And what is his definition of magic, "The knowledge of knowing."

PLACES

Las Vegas has it all..Oscar Goodman, Mayor of Las Vegas

I Say Haunted, And You Say Hoopla

Las Vegas is convention goers in cheap suits, grannies clutching cups of coins, cocktail waitresses with legs up to here, bronzed and buff bodybuilders and high rollers with their deep pockets and silicone enhanced trophy wives. And the stars, the rising stars, the falling stars, those that aspire to stardom, and those that never quite made it but keep on hoping nonetheless. This city long ago eclipsed Hollywood as the entertainment capital of the world. It's the see-and-be-seen city.

But there's another side to the city. People live here, work here, and die here. Some of those who live here do so with the ghosts of those who've decided to stick around long after the Grim Reaper's come calling. Such is the case of Brit and Lang Bolan.

Theirs is a brand new house; built in the midst of frenzied buyers' market the likes of which may never be seen again. The pseudo, early California stucco, sits on a postage stamp size lot in a neighborhood of cul-de-sacs, squat palm trees, and other cookie-cutter dwellings. This is the new Las Vegas, a middle-class mecca of swimming pools that glisten in backyard, after backyard, after backyard.

Certainly the pools are status symbols, but necessary nonetheless. It gets damn hot here on the tip of the Mojave desert, but not too hot for a haunting. Brit and Lang are proud of the home they've lived in only a short while. And yet, this house, with all its modern up-to-the-minute, middle-class trappings, is the residence of a ghostly little girl.

They have seen her walk across the tile floors and right through their living room wall. They call her "Irene." And explain that the name is as good as any other. Neither Brit nor Lang seems to indulge in flights of fancy. She's a swing shift pit boss at one of the mega-resort hotel casinos and he's a graveyard bartender. It works for them.

Like so many Las Vegans they've both been on the marriage-go-round before. Between them, they've racked up five previous marriages. This time, they say, is for keeps. And judging by the way they lovingly stare at each another, you want to believe.

Brit is an exceptionally attractive woman, tall, tan and model skinny. Her long, silver blonde streaked hair catches and reflects the sunlight. Take twenty years from her and she could be strutting her stuff with the best of them up at the Ghost Bar, or any other young singles gathering place. Lang is obviously several years younger than Brit. His dark good looks are the perfect contrast to his wife.

Brit wears vintage clothing and collects antique furniture. She points a freshly manicured, rose pink nail toward a maple armoire.

"We've been wondering if maybe Irene didn't hitch a ride here in some of the furniture. We bought the armoire as a housewarming gift to ourselves...."

Lang picks up the story from his wife. "We've heard that ghosts can become attached to personal possessions... But we've also wondered if she isn't the member of a pioneer family that passed this way a long time ago. Maybe she died in the desert and her family buried her somewhere around here."

Both agree that the stringy haired ghost girl doesn't bother them

"Some people might think I'd have a difficult time sleeping by myself knowing there's a ghost in the house." Brit says. "Not in the least. I come home from work, I read an hour or two, watch a little tv and I'm ready to call it a day."

Lang laughs. "But that wasn't so the first time you saw her."

Brit nods in agreement. "We'd only been in the house about a week. Lang was at work and I was unpacking some of my Depression glass. I noticed movement across the room and thought it was the dog. I looked up and saw this little girl walking across the floor. My heart started beating a mile a minute. She was dressed in old time clothes and I knew…I just knew she was a ghost. She walked right through the wall. I didn't get a wink of sleep until Lang came home at nine."

They both laugh at the memory. Then Brit adds, "I was so scared. I almost called Lang and asked him to take an EO!" *

Lang lovingly rests his hand on his wife's shoulder.

"We thought about a ghost investigation …but decided against it. We know she means us no harm, and we can live with her. "

* EO is known in Nevada casino employee parlance as an Early Out. An employee that wishes to leave before his/her shift is completed asks for an "EO"

Clark County Museum

If any place is going to be haunted it stands to reason that place might be a museum. After all, museums are the repositories for the belongings and personal effects of people long dead. Not to be missed by either the history buff or the ghosthunter is the Clark County Museum in Henderson. Here you will find exhibits displayed in a somewhat unique setting.

Visiting Heritage Street at the museum is like stepping back in time. The main exhibits here are historic houses set on this shady street that looks like Main Street USA circa 1940-1950. And that's the whole idea. The houses were rescued from various locations throughout the Las Vegas area and brought here to be renovated and filled with items from the specific era the home depicts.

The Beckley House is a Craftsman bungalow that was built sometime in the 1920's by Jake and Leva Beckley. Most of the furnishings in the house were those of Mr. and Mrs. Beckley who lived in the house until their deaths.
Go ahead step inside the Beckley House. You almost expect to hear some sit-com dad from the fifties calling, "Honey. I'm home!"

What you hear may not be the sit-com dad after all. Some of the houses are said to the residences of a ghost or two. Former owners? Perhaps! But who can say for sure?

A few years ago my nephew Dalvante Hursh accompanied by his grandmother and grandfather visited the museum. While in the Giles/Barcus House his grandmother explained how different life had been back then. But something else held Dalvante's attention. He didn't like the house and liked what he saw even less.

Finally he said, "I want to go."

"But why?" His grandmother asked.

The little boy shrugged and pointed to something only he saw. "Because!"

Thinking that he needed a nap, Dalvante's grandparents agreed to leave. Later he would explain that he just didn't like the house. He is not alone in this. Other children have felt similar "strangeness" in some of the houses on Heritage Street.

Author's nephew Dalvante Hursh points to the Giles/Barcus House

In the Beckley house reported sightings include an elderly man and a ghostly little girl who stands near the staircase that leads to the attic. There also seems to be a prank playing spirit in residence. Unseen hands sometimes muss the bed. One minute the bedspread is nice and neat, the next it is rumpled. Museum employees are at a loss to explain how this occurs.

When recently asked about his trip to the Giles/Barcus House, Dalvante had forgotten most of what happened except for the fact that he was "kinda scared that day"."

The Giles/Barcus House was originally built in Goldfield in 1905; Edwin Schofield Giles and his wife Edith Corliss Giles purchased it in 1928. Their daughter Edith Giles Barcus brought the house to Las Vegas in 1955. It sat on the corner of Hacienda and Giles Streets where it served as an antique store for many years.

At the Goumond House the apparition of a young woman has been seen standing in the doorway, and a large ghostly black cat is sometimes spotted scampering down the hallway.

As they do in many haunted houses, doors open and shut of their own volition. But most of the strange activity seems to center around the sewing room where ceiling lights have been broken in their sockets and an iron was once flung from the ironing board.

I recently visited the museum with a friend who is a sensitive. While we didn't find anything unusual, she felt that that paranormal activity might be connected in some way to the child's room in Townsite House; it was here that she picked up a strong feeling of sadness.

Others who wandered in and out of the houses that day seemed to be oblivious to anything out of the ordinary. But then perhaps they weren't really looking.

Dresser in the bedroom of the Goumond House

The Las Vegas Academy

Razing remodeling and bulldozing has become a way of life in the city that continually re-invents itself. Thankfully area historians have stepped in to protect what's left of the city's heritage; a few old buildings are still standing. One of these survivors happens to be the oldest high school in the city.

The school's main building was built at 315 S. 7th Street in 1931. Formerly known as Las Vegas High, the school was renamed the Las Vegas Academy of International Studies, Performing and Visual Arts in 1994.

Stories of the ghost who has taken up residence in the schools auditorium have been popular with students for years.

This spirit catches the blame for cold breezes, doors that slam for no reason, misplaced items and an occasional power outage. The specter, some say, is a former teacher, a long dead student, or a man who lived and died near the spot the school was built upon. Whoever he was in life, death seems to have given the ghost a chance to revel in the limelight; his favorite place is onstage.

Not everyone is convinced the building is haunted. One person who works in the building insists there is absolutely no ghostly activity going on here. Others say there is definitely a presence in the building.

Treem Elementary School

Here's to the ivy covered walls and the old alma mater. Schools are favorite locations for ghostly goings on. Not all schoolyard specters are former students. Often the ghost that haunts a particular school may never have actually set foot in the building.

Take the case of the crying ghost girl who occasionally appears on the school grounds at Treem Elementary School in Henderson. Some of those who've seen her describe a young girl dressed in pioneer garb of the mid 1800's. Others say that her face is the only distinguishable feature about her.

It's possible she was a member of an emigrant family that crossed the Southern Nevada area more than a century ago; she may have died along the way and was buried in an unmarked grave. Perhaps her story is more sinister. The ghostly crying child might be the victim of a long ago murder, still seeking revenge.

Sparring Specters

Till death do you part...Encouraging words added to many a marriage ceremony. But what if the spouses have decided not to let death part them and cease their marital spats?

The raucous bickering of a long dead couple occasionally echoes through this older home in the valley late at night. They lived here decades ago, one followed the other to the grave in a matter of days; the marriage is thought to have been a happy one, and yet... the fights continue. The home's owners claim it cannot be defined as haunted because the ghostly arguments are heard only sporadically, and then not by everyone.

When a jealous husband shot and killed his erring wife and then turned the gun on himself, he couldn't have known that they would continue to haunt the small house they called home.

Decades after the murderous rampage neighborhood teenagers still believed the house was haunted. Tenants moved in; tenants moved out. Some claimed to have heard a terrible argument between a ghostly man and a woman; others saw a crying woman walking down the hall. The majority of tenants simply didn't like the house.

A Shot in the Dark

The world lived by a more rigid code of conduct in the 1950's. Men were expected to be gentlemen at all times and women were to be ladies no matter what.

She was a waitress at one of the local eateries. He was a card dealer at a downtown Fremont Street casino. They were adults, divorced and lonely. When they met it was by chance; he stopped in for a quick meal before heading home to his lonely apartment, gave her the once over and she responded in kind. Within the week they were dating. A month later they were meeting at the home he'd once shared with his ex-wife.

Soon they fell into a routine. They drank, made love, and drank some more; on occasion they quarreled. Their arguments were nothing serious, certainly nothing like the acrimonious battles they'd shared with their long gone spouses. Until the night she really made him mad.

Naked or not, she had to be locked out of the house. So he shoved her out the back door and bolted it shut. Silently he listened at the door as she begged him to let her in or at least toss out her clothes. She could beg all she wanted. He wasn't about to do either. His ex-wife might have warned her that he hung onto his anger longer than most; her ex might have warned him that she was relentless when it came to getting her own way.

There was a gun in the glove compartment of the friend's car she had borrowed. She skulked out to the car and returned to the door with the gun. Thinking that the gun would be just as good a key as anything else, she took aim at the lock and fired. Unfortunately her erstwhile lover had chosen that moment to listen at the door; the bullet struck him just below the heart. He was dead and she was later arrested on a charge of involuntary manslaughter. Propriety first and foremost, she was properly attired when the first police office arrived on the scene.

Saucers over Sin City

Area 51 and Groom Lake aside, there have been many strange sightings reported in the Southern Nevada desert. None are stranger than that witnessed by three tourists enroute to Las Vegas decades ago.

As their car sped down the lonely highway the sun dropped into the horizon and the sky turned from deep rich purple to pitch black. A sliver of moon crested the hills, but they hardly noticed as they joked about the bundle each hoped to win in what they affectionately referred to as "Lost Wages."

They rode in companionable silence awhile; then the subject of dinner came up. While they discussed the specialties of different casino coffee shops, a bright light flashed in the distance and something caught their eyes. All three gazed in amazement at what they would later describe as a shiny smooth flying saucer. The object seemed to be hovering near Las Vegas.

"What in the world?" The driver asked his passengers.
"Looks like some sort of flying saucer!"
"Maybe it's a new sign they're putting up in Las Vegas."
"No. It's some sort of--" He hesitated. "It's a flying saucer all right!"

And then as quickly as it had appeared, the dome shaped craft vanished.

Had they seen a ghostly craft from another galaxy, time travelers from our own planet, or just some weird desert mirage? The three witnesses weren't sure what it was, but they knew it was not like anything they'd ever seen before.

Within a few years there would be more reports of strange craft and weird lights in the skies over Las Vegas. One witness would describe something like a giant string of white lights hovering over Sunrise Mountain.

Nellis Air Force Base

Deep within the confines of Nellis Air Force Base is the mysterious Area 51 Groom Lake. No one, other than authorized personnel, is permitted access. No one! The compound is impenetrable; any place off site that might afford a view belongs to the federal government and is also off limits. Warning signs are clearly posted, and armed guards reconnoiter the entire area. Trespassers are arrested.

UFO's, aliens, and secret government experiments have long been rumored to be the reason for such guarded secrecy.

That's not all the strange goings on that happens here. According to some, a few ghosts haunt Nellis Air Force Base. A ghostly gray man has been seen in certain hangars. He is believed to be an unfortunate airman who lost his life in a jet crash decades ago. In yet another hangar unexplained laughter and moaning can occasionally be heard.

Carluccios Tivoli Gardens

Carluccios Tivoli Gardens serves up some of the finest Italian cuisine in town. Located at 1775 E. Tropicana Ave., the restaurant once belonged to Liberace. The flamboyant entertainer loved his Tivoli Gardens and spent many happy times here between his engagements at the local hotel/casinos. Whenever the chance presented itself, he entertained other celebrities at his restaurant.

Liberace wanted a showplace where patrons could enjoy not only the ambiance, but superb food as well. He helped plan the menus and did much of the interior decorating. When time permitted, he couldn't resist dropping in to play a few tunes on the piano. As might be expected, these impromptu appearances delighted diners.

After Liberace's death in 1989 Carluccios took over the Tivoli Gardens and strange things started happening. Some suspect that the ghostly Mr. Showmanship still drops in from time to time just to see how things are going. His apparition usually appears in a sequined accented tuxedo and smiles warmly at those who see him. A patron told the following story.

"We'd just finished our dinner. I looked up and saw a Liberace lookalike smile at me then sit down at the piano. 'Is he taking requests?' I asked the server.

'Who?' The server asked.

'That man at the piano.' I said nodding toward the piano. That's when I noticed that no one was sitting at the piano.

When the server told me that they had no piano player that night I felt a cold chill run up my back.

It's no coincidence that Carluccios is in the same shopping center as the Liberace Museum; at one time the entertainer had plans to build a complete Liberace plaza at the center. The museum houses many of his costumes, pianos and other items. Perhaps it is all these personal effects that draw the ghostly Liberace. Then again he could be exercising a star's prerogative to see that the show goes on.

Orbs in Carluccios on the night of the séance

Sin City Séance 2: Looking for Liberace

On a recent warm summer evening participants gathered for a ghost investigation/séance at Carluccios. The atmosphere was charged with anticipation and excitement; we set up cameras and meters and as the dowsers proceeded to seek evidence of Liberace's continued existence, master magician and medium Dixie Dooley put items on the séance table. Candles, a crystal ball, a slate, a bell, and a tambourine were placed on the table in hopes that Liberace might avail himself of at least one of them.

As Dixie checked to make sure there was no trickery afoot, I wondered if the spirit of Liberace would actually ring the bell. Perhaps one of us who sat around the table would glimpse a vision of the pianist in the depths of the crystal ball. Maybe he'd blow out the candles, write something on the slate, or pound out a message with the tambourine.

The dowsers had located two areas of the room where activity might occur, and we were ready to begin. Thousands of tiny white lights twinkled overhead, reflections sparkled in the mirrors and the candles were flickering ever so slightly. This is an enchanting room; will Liberace join us?

Dixie explains there is no guarantee that the entertainer will answer our summons and invites those who knew

Liberace in life to share their memories. We join hands; Dixie begins to call for Liberace. Our eyes are closed, we focus all our concentration upon him. We open our eyes and each of us gazes into the crystal ball. Candlelight dances across it, no Liberace. His theme song was *I'll Be Seeing You,* but on this night he will not be joining us from the hereafter.

As we prepare to leave someone mentions the two tall communications towers located behind Carluccios. Are these towers haunted? There is a rumor that those who work on the towers will only do so during daylight hours. No doubt there are many explanations for this. But then again.....

Las Vegas Villa

Liberace kept his audiences enthralled with his musical genius and his outlandish stage attire, the more sequins, feathers and flash, the better. Like the fans of Elvis, Liberace's adored him. He was Mr. Showmanship; Las Vegas embraced him and claimed him as its own. For his part, Liberace owed many fabulous homes in other cities, but thought of Las Vegas as home.

His home at 4982 Shirley Ave. is known today as Las Vegas Villa. Situated in a middle class neighborhood, it probably is not the sort of place one might think of as a star's residence. But indeed Liberace lived here for many years. The home is actually two houses that were converted into a fabulous showplace fit for Mr. Showmanship. Inside are priceless objects d' art, and other ostentatious trappings. The master bathroom is as big as most people's living rooms; its centerpiece is a pillared sunken marble bathtub, overhead an exquisite crystal chandelier.

Money was no object and no expense was spared. In the master bedroom a million-dollar replica of the Sistine Chapel was painted on the ceiling; a descendant of Michelangelo did the exquisite work.

Some people have flair. They know how to live life to  its most lavish extremes. Of course, just knowing is not enough; one must also be able to afford the costly accouterments that make up such a lavish lifestyle. As one of Las Vegas' highest paid superstars, Liberace was such a person.

Those who wish to take a peek at such grandeur will be happy to know that weddings and other special events can be booked at Las Vegas Villa. The ghostly Liberace is said to make visits to his former residence on occasion. A woman, who toured the Villa, related the following incident.

"I was standing a yard or so from the water fountain when I noticed a stream of silvery blue water spiraling down from the ceiling. As I watched the water cascade to the floor, I told myself to be careful not to slip in the small puddle that was forming. How could that water be coming from the ceiling, I wondered. I glanced away for a moment trying to figure out how it was connected to the water fountain.

When I looked back the stream of water was gone. The floor was dry and there was no puddle. I looked up and saw the blue painting of Liberace's face on the ceiling (see photo above.) It was exactly where the stream of water had come from!"

Fountain in Las Vegas Villa

Liberace's Bedroom at Las Vegas Villa   Roy Harper

There are those who believe that the ghostly Liberace is still very much in residence at his Shirley Avenue home.

Liberace's living room

Your Waiter is a Wraith

Don't you want to know
why the rain tastes of Merlot?

Todd and Carla discovered the elegant little restaurant by chance. They'd spent a grueling afternoon looking at new cars, comparing sticker prices, and options. When hunger struck, it hit hard.

New cars were forgotten for the time being as they went in search of a place to eat. Fast food was fine for their workday fare, but it was the weekend and they wanted something nicer, something with soup and salad, candles flickering, music and a wine list that offered more than red or white.

They found it at the restaurant that quickly became their favorite. By the time they purchased their new car, they'd fallen into the routine of starting each weekend with dinner here. Their dining pleasure was further enhanced by the capable service of their favorite waiter Enrique.

Always jovial, he regaled them with the latest kitchen gossip while seeing to their every need. True or not, these tidbits were lighthearted and entertaining. But Enrique was first and foremost a topnotch waiter; he remembered their favorite dishes, and knew what specials, or new dishes to suggest. After a meal was concluded, he invariably presented the dessert tray with a flourish and the words, "What is life without our sweet little sins?"

Occasionally they agreed and hungrily dove into thick slabs of New York style Cheesecake topped with glazed raspberries. Most of the time they declined with a chuckle. "Well we won't be sinning tonight."

Their schedules changed and the Friday night ritual of dining at the restaurant ended. Months went by. When they again found themselves sharing a Friday night off they decided to celebrate by dining at their favorite restaurant.
No one in the place seemed to be smiling; the maitre d that usually seated them so cheerfully was sullen. He led them to a corner table and skulked away silently. They

glanced at their menu, then scanned the room for Enrique who was nowhere in sight.

"Chef must be in a very sour mood tonight." Carla said absently.

"Either that, or someone lost a bundle at the tables," Todd smiled, remembering Enrique's tale of those on the staff who liked to bet big at Blackjack.

"Oh look thcre's Enrique now." Carla said waving to the waiter who stood across the room from them.

"I don't think he saw you." Todd said.

At that moment Enrique approached their table. Without smiling or acknowledging them, the waiter slowly turned and walked in the other direction. He stopped, absently wiped a table with his snow-white towel, and then headed toward the kitchen.

"Now I know what a rebuff is." Todd laughed. "I wonder what his problem is."

"I don't know. Maybe a love affair gone awry." Carla surmised jokingly.

Soon another waiter was at the table. He filled their water goblets and said, "Good evening, my name is Philipe and I will be your server tonight. May I suggest the Veal Piccatta or--"

Todd didn't let him finish his well rehearsed spiel. "Aren't we sitting in Enrique's section?"

Philipe nodded somberly that it was so.

"We just saw him headed toward the kitchen. Will you kindly ask him to come out here and wait on us?"

"I am so sorry sir but---"

Carla interrupted. "What is wrong? Everyone, even Enrique, seems to be in a bad mood tonight!"

The waiter motioned to the maitre d who came running.

"They saw Enrique going into the kitchen." Philipe told him.

The maitre d sternly looked first at Carla then at Todd. "I am afraid that is quite impossible!"

"Well just go in the kitchen and---" Carla demanded.

"Madam! Enrique was killed in a car accident yesterday in Seattle."

Both Carla and Todd shivered as cold chills rushed through them. They had seen Enrique, but saw no need to pursue the argument. After apologies all around, they decided against dinner and went home to ponder how strange life can be.

Oasis Motel

Why would someone with talent and looks and everything to live for suddenly end it all in a strange hotel room in Las Vegas? Actor David Strickland who played an art critic in the hit TV series *Suddenly Susan* did just that on a Monday night in March 1999.

Strickland checked into his room at the Oasis Motel, early in the afternoon. Sometime between then and the next morning he tore the bed sheets into strips and fashioned a rope. Looping it over the ceiling beam, he knotted a noose around his neck. His lifeless body was discovered by a motel employee early Tuesday morning. According to newspaper reports, Strickland was due in a Los Angeles court to answer charges of illegal drug use that very morning.

Whatever his reasons, David Strickland was not the first person to commit suicide at the hotel. Perhaps this accounts for the sounds of weeping and footsteps that are said to be heard in certain rooms. On occasion an unexplained cold spot is also said to envelop a certain corner of the room.

Orbit Inn

The Orbit Inn was located at 707 E. Fremont Street in the downtown area favored by those who preferred it to the flashier strip. A million-dollar motel, the Orbit Inn was modern, chrome and glass with 147 rooms. There was also a small casino with several slot machines and a few table games.

On Saturday night January 7 1967 a young man and his wife checked into the Orbit Inn. To the clerk who assigned them room 214 on the second floor, they seemed to be like any other couple who came through the door, out for a weekend of good times and gambling. They weren't.

The man held a terrible secret. He was set to carry out a cruel plan, a plan that would leave him, his wife, and four other people dead. Hidden in his luggage were ten sticks of dynamite and a gun. No one will ever know the reasons behind the murder/suicide plot, or just what he and his wife discussed in their last hours of life. It's doubtful she had any inkling of her fate.

At 1:30 in the morning he fired the gun that detonated his homemade bomb; the ensuing blast rocked the downtown area.

Windows were shattered for blocks. The scene was one of horror; many of the victims were dismembered. A human head was thrust into an alley across from the motel. A leg was embedded in a concrete wall and a woman's hand still wearing a wedding ring was located near the rubble.

Medley of Mishaps

If you live in a brand new house, condo or apartment yet sometimes have the strangest feeling that your abode is haunted, it well could be. Your home may be 21st century new, but the land it sits upon is as old as the earth itself. What weird things occurred on that land or in the area 100 years ago? Or even 50 years ago? Is it possible that the remnants of some tragic event played out decades ago still lingers? Do the ghosts of those who discovered too late that tempting fate is seldom wise haunt certain places?

Death Defying Dive

A young man attempted to defy the odds by diving into the shimmering swimming pool from the balcony of his ultra modern second floor apartment. Proud of his successful dive, he jumped out of the pool, ran back up the stairs and stunned onlookers for the second time with another flawless swan dive.

As any gambler knows luck can change in an instant. Instead of walking away the winner in his weird game of chance, he stood poised on the balcony set to dive into the pool for the third time. But this time his luck ran out; he miscalculated the distance and was killed instantly when he landed headfirst onto the cement of the swimming pool area…

Road Kill Revenge

Years ago an elderly man and his wife were driving along a lonely highway outside of Las Vegas. They'd enjoyed their annual vacation to the Desert City and were engrossed in plans for next year's jaunt when their car suddenly smashed into something. Pulling to the shoulder of the road he got out to see what he'd hit. A dying cow lay in the road. As he stood staring down at the pitiful animal a large truck came barreling down the highway toward him.

Frantic that her husband might be killed, the woman jumped out of the car and waved her arms wildly in warning to the truck. The truck driver tried desperately to brake and avoid the man in the middle of the road. Unfortunately he could not prevent his truck from sliding into the man and killing him…

Best Laid Plans

He knew this road better than anyone; he had driven over it countless times. Traffic was lighter than usual on this night; he allowed his mind to wonder as he drove past familiar sights. Lost in thought, he paid little attention to the car in front of him; until the crunch of his vehicle rear-ending its bumper jarred him back to the present.

It was nothing more than a minor fender bender, a nuisance that might make him a few minutes late for his date. But he could explain. Almost cheerfully, he jumped out to inspect the damage. An exchange of names and driver's license numbers and he would be on his way. He spoke to other driver who remained in his vehicle. While he compared his bumper to that of the other car, a third car came careening around the corner. Before he could jump to safety the speeding car smashed into him tossing his body 20 feet in the air. He was dead before the ambulance arrived...

Heartbreak

They were young, and married and the parents of a baby girl. He worked as a police officer at Nellis Air Force Base. She was a housewife. Her days were spent cleaning, and cooking and taking care of their baby. It was the early 1950's; this was the accepted norm.

Like all young couples they enjoyed an occasional night out. With Helldorado in full force, they hired a babysitter and joined the fun loving crowd downtown. Hours later they returned home, paid the babysitter and prepared for bed.

Waken by the sound of her parents' laughter, the toddler started to whimper. Her mother cradled her lovingly and attempted to rock her back to sleep. The baby's father sat directly across from them loading his gun. He was a police officer. He knew about burglars, robbers and killers. His family would be protected.

Then, without warning, the gun discharged. A bullet struck the baby in the forehead, just missing its mother. Frozen in horror, the young man could do nothing but stare. One long, loud, agonizing scream escaped from his wife. Alarmed by the noise, neighbors came running. An ambulance was called, and the fatally wounded child was rushed to a nearby hospital. He crawled under the bed and refused to come out until police threatened him with tear gas. The child's death was found to be a tragic accident…

Drum Roll for the Disembodied

Are ghosts responsible for the strange events that occur in life?

Change the Subject

When the police pulled him over, the young AWOL serviceman was driving erratically. He was also behind the wheel of a stolen car. This fact got him arrested. Police work in the 1950's was not high tech. Unaided by databases and computers, it took a few days for them to discover that the owner of the stolen car was in California. Dead of massive head injuries, his body had lain a week in his small home.

Before he was extradited, the young man was questioned. Why? Why kill someone just to steal a car? His reply was swift. It was not so much the car he wanted, as it was silence. It was all this talk of ghosts. He explained that he had just gotten sick and tired of the victim's incessant talk of ghosts and disembodied spirits…

Stalking Specter

He went to the police department with a serious complaint. For some unknown reason someone was following him everywhere he went, and he wanted it stopped. After careful questioning, the police determined that no one was following the man. Perhaps he could find some answers at the mental health facility.

No! He would stop the person that tagged behind him one way or the other. He found that way one morning on the highway between Boulder City and Las Vegas. As the truck approached, he waved madly to the driver. Before the driver could react, he dove under the truck, killing himself and putting an end to his torment.

All My Worldly Possessions

It was Thanksgiving Day. All across the city people gathered before their televisions and their roast turkey dinners. Many casino workers hurriedly ate their turkey in employee cafeterias, and rushed back on to the floor. The gambling public must be served, holiday or not.

He was alone on this holiday. Without family or friends, the elderly man decided to take his own life. Whatever his reasons, when he left this world, it wasn't without a will.

All his worldly possessions, and explicit instructions for his funeral, were left to the Las Vegas Police Chief. And while his bodied awaited burial in the city morgue, there was talk of strange occurrences in the jail. Unexplained cold drafts and mumbling voices led some to believe the jail just might be haunted.

Red Mill Melody

¿Soy muerto?

Sí. `

No le creo!

Opening night at the Moulin Rouge 1955. The body of a young saxophonist was discovered in a field less than a mile from the famed nightclub and hotel. His neck was broken the result of a fall during a wild party of alcohol and drugs. But the show must go on. A suitable replacement was found, and the saxophone player was all but forgotten.

It mattered little that the young man had worked so hard to get here. Life is for the living. So celebrities and notables of the day came and went. And the opening celebrations went forward.

The Moulin Rouge has been closed many years. Yet some have heard the sounds of laughter, and of music, and a saxophone solo that could knock your socks off, coming from the deserted building late at night. Could it be a spectral saxophonist determined to grab just one more moment in the spotlight?

Benny Binion statue downtown Las Vegas

Binion Haunts

Criminal past in Texas or not, this town loved gambling pioneer, Benny Binion. He and his family owned and operated the Horseshoe Casino for over 40 years. Binion

117

was good to his employees. And they in turn were loyal to him. An innovator, Binion was the first to offer high stakes betting and poker tournaments at his Horseshoe. His was also the first casino to add wall to wall carpeting.

Benny Binion is long dead. His beloved Horseshoe is no longer owned and operated by his family. Money woes. His son Ted died under mysterious circumstances; he is at the center of a murder trial that has rocked Las Vegas. Will the truth ever come to light? Was Ted the victim of foul play or did an accidental drug overdose do him in?

Decades ago a Binion employee was murdered in the parking garage. Rumor was he'd neglected to repay a loan with the wrong person. Unaware, that he is dead, the man's confused specter has been seen wandering the garage many times since that night.

He is not the only ghost connected to the Binion name. The old family house on Bonanza Road is boarded up and forgotten, a reminder of how things were in the Las Vegas of years ago. The house is haunted, some say.

Details on the ghostly activity are sketchy. Mysterious lights, a shadowing figure that stands at the upstairs window and children's laughter echoing across the lot have been reported.

Neon Nocturne

She is silver.
And she comes through my window
with the moonlight.

Rita grew up in her grandparents' house on the Westside. The elderly couple raised her while her mother worked as a maid in one of the big hotels downtown. Until her sixteenth birthday, Rita saw her mother only as a woman so stooped and exhausted, she barely had the energy to even speak.

On that night she began to understand her mother.

After the cake and ice cream, Rita's grandmother scrubbed her tiny kitchen clean. Satisfied that everything was in order, she kissed Rita then shuffled down the hall towards her bedroom. When the door was closed Rita's mother grabbed her hand. "I've got something to tell you about your daddy!"

It happened so long ago. The pain in her mother's eyes was as alive as if it had been only yesterday. Suddenly Rita realized the reason for her mother's quiet sadness all those years. It hadn't been the demands of being a hotel maid at all. Life and all its cruelties were to blame for this zombie she called mama.

Her mother spoke in a rush. "Extra money! Your daddy took that night cashier job so that we would have extra money...So we could afford a bigger place. There we were. Not knowing a soul. But he had always dreamed of living in Los Angeles so that's where we were. Some teenagers came into the store that night, high on some drug or other. Waving guns around, they told your daddy to give them everything in the cash drawer. He was always so stubborn...He refused to give them anything and they shot him. Four times."

Long after the lights were out, Rita cried for the woman she'd never understood until this night. It was a beginning and an end. Her mother would be dead within the year.

At twenty-one, Rita was beautiful and headstrong, and spoiled. She drove a brand new car and her wardrobe was the envy of every woman in the neighborhood. Her grandmother was pampered with new furniture and appliances. Why not? She was making a very good living as a cocktail waitress.

With her grandfather dead, the house was too quiet. Rita had always taken comfort in the petty bickering of the old couple. Now the afternoons held either silence or the noise of daytime television.

But life was looking up for Rita. A new boyfriend, a new job and then... One night she was alive and serving drinks, the next she was just another body in the desert....A beautiful woman in a shimmering green dress has been spotted near downtown casinos in the early morning hours. If anyone should speak to her, she turns and dissolves into the night.

Song of Suicide

Suzanne pulls the cover back and peers out at the night.

Is this what is meant by being completely free?   Unheard, unseen, unfelt.

She walks across the darkness...............

If you are with us Suzanne please give us a sign!

Unheard,   unseen, unfelt.

We really want to make contact with you, Suz---

Suicide is a fact of life. The taking of one's own life is a quick way out of problems, real and imagined. An escape, if you will. An escape that leaves behind broken hearts and unanswered questions.

Nevada does not lead the nation in suicide. Neither does Las Vegas. And yet, this city, sparkling with so much promise, is the final destination for some of those wishing to end it all. Perhaps it is the city's allure. After all, there is no place on earth quite like Las Vegas.

Obviously Hotels/Casinos spokespersons are reluctant to talk about the suicides that have occurred on their property....

In the past ten years three people have gone the top of the Stratosphere and dove headlong onto the street below. At the Luxor a man decided to jump from the 8th floor down into the casino. A distraught young woman leapt to her death from the 9th floor of a casino parking garage. Others shoot, poison, or hang themselves out of this world. Where there's a will, there's a way....And the hauntings continue...

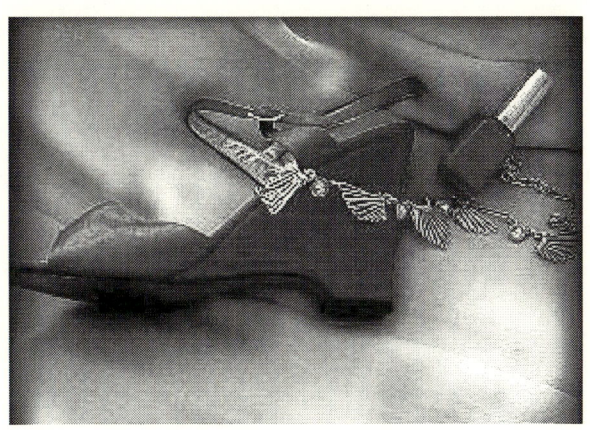

Sin City Serenade

It's madness to think that I should be banished from this
place where moonlight caresses marble angel wings.
And shadows dance across filigree iron gates.
Go toward the light...demand their arrogant whispers.

Prostitution is legal in Nevada. However, it is illegal in Clark County; this effectively makes the oldest profession against the law in Las Vegas, the county seat for Clark County. But everyone has to eat. And ladies still ply their trade throughout the city. Some are flagrant, most carry on clandestinely. Illegal drugs, assault, robbery, you name it; numerous crimes are associated with illegal prostitution. This of course, keeps vice officers busy.

Occasionally a young woman dies at the hands of a violent customer. Experienced women generally develop the uncanny ability to spot the violent ones. But not always. Those who are new to the business learn to access character in a matter of seconds. If she is wrong, a woman will pay for the mistake with a beating, or death if she isn't so lucky.

Mandy was a sixteen year old runaway. Nothing her mother said made sense to her anymore. She worked long hours just to feed Mandy and her kid sister; when she wasn't waiting tables at the diner, she went on and on and on about the importance of an education. If she was so smart why didn't she have one? Mandy finally got tired of listening to her mother, and of taking orders from her. So she fled the small town in Ohio for the bright lights of Vegas.

Mandy took a job at a fast food restaurant; within a month she had discovered a better paying job in the world of prostitution. It was almost too easy. With her make-up on she looked older than her sixteen years, much older. This, and her fake ID, enabled her to successfully pass as an adult in hotel bars and lounges along the strip.

The money! She'd never seen so much money. For the first time in her life Mandy could buy things. Clothes and shoes and a computer and video games and.......... She wanted it all. Her plans included sending money home for her mother and her sister. Eventually she would share her newfound wealth. Eventually.

He noticed her as soon as she walked into the lounge. She smiled. He was interested. They chatted. And a deal was struck. Other, more experienced women may have pegged him for the violent sort. Not Mandy. His smile was disarming. Besides, he was offering her more money to spend the night with him than her mother made in a month.

It made her careless. Not wise enough to look beyond dollar signs, the teenager agreed to go with him to his room. Sometime between their meeting at the bar and their arrival at his hotel room on the strip, Mandy was savagely beaten to death. Hotel personnel discovered her battered body the next day.

When he was apprehended, the killer supplied few details to the girl's murder, other than the fact he was guilty of it.

An unexplained cold spot in an otherwise comfortably warm hotel room, the television is off, likewise the radio, and yet the occasional sound of soft weeping. An echo from the past. What transpired in this room yesterday, a week ago, last month, or a year ago?

Lake Mead

With Hoover Dam completed, the waters from the Colorado began to spill over and fill Lake Mead; the towns of St. Thomas, Callville and Rioville were flooded and eventually covered by the waters. Those who lived in St. Thomas worked at a feverish pace to relocate their cemetery to Overton, while lumber and other valuable building materials were removed.

Then on June 11,1938 the waters rushed in. The three towns were completely submerged beneath 100 feet of water. When the area is severely drought ridden Lake Mead recedes and remnants of St. Thomas can be seen. According to some, this is when a ghostly young lady slowly walks among the ruins of the old water sodden ghost towns.

Surrounded by a richly colored landscape, Lake Mead sparkles in the hot afternoon sun, belying the many tragedies and deaths that have occurred beneath its surface. Plane crashes, boating accidents and drowning have claimed the lives of several people since the lake was created. Most of their bodies have been recovered. Some have been lost to the lake's murky depths.

The largest manmade lake in the United States, it is a popular recreational spot for Nevada and Arizona boaters, water skiers, and swimmers. More than a million tourists visit the lake and the Lake Mead Recreation Area annually.

On a quiet night, with moonlight glistening across the lake's surface, it's easy enough to believe that yes, this body of water is indeed haunted.

Crash

April 21 1958.... Springtime in the desert, not a cloud in the sky. A student pilot and his instructor take off from Nellis Air Force Base in the F-100F jet. In Los Angeles forty-seven people board a DC-7 bound for New York. Within the hour all would be dead...

An elderly couple working in their garden heard the sound of a terrible explosion; looking toward the desert, they saw the gray white puff of smoke. A local casino owner set out in his private plane for an early morning flight over the Las Vegas Valley. Suddenly a mayday called rattled on his radio. He looked out and saw pieces of wreckage fluttering to earth.

Twelve miles south of Las Vegas the fighter jet collided with the airliner; the ensuing wreckage would be strewn over several miles. Sixteen years earlier actress Carole Lombard had lost her life in a plane crash in the same vicinity.

As the bodies were recovered they were taken by military ambulance to a makeshift mortuary at the old Las Vegas racetrack. Las Vegas was smaller then. There were only three funeral homes in town. As one newspaper of the day reported, "Morticians from all three funeral homes appeared with cases of embalming fluid..........."

Within the year new flight patterns and regulations would be in place for Nellis Air Force Base jets and all other aircraft, private and commercial. Never again would such a tragedy be allowed to occur.

Progress has overtaken the valley. Highways and freeways, shopping malls, schools, fast food restaurants, and new homes now stand on land that was once covered with sagebrush and yucca.

It happened at the Coroner's

We're all a bit curious as to the inner workings of the coroner's office. Think not? Then why the popularity of television shows like CSI Las Vegas, Miami, and New York?

Extraordinary things do occur at the coroner's little corner of the universe. Here is where mysteries are hopefully explained, and law enforcement personnel are aided in the solving of crimes. Hopefully.

Unless one dies of some catastrophic illness in a hospital bed, chances are good he, or she, will make a personal appearance at the coroner's. Famous and dead, or dead, broke and unknown, it make's no difference. Hundreds of bodies arrive at the Clark County Coroner's office each year. Most of those are autopsied and sent on their way. Occasionally something bizarre happens. The following incident is an example.

While working on a large gasoline tank, a man removed his oxygen mask, complained of feeling sick stumbled and fell 40 feet to his death in the tank.

It was an hour before the body could be retrieved and taken to the coroner's. There it was left overnight in the refrigerator, a matter of routine. Next day as the autopsy began; noxious fumes arose from the body.

The coroner's office was evacuated and closed for the day, until a hazardous material team could come in and make certain there was no longer any danger to the living. When it was safe, it was business as usual.

Chasin' Down an Urban Legend

Urban legends and ghost stories. Every city has them. Over time the two may blend together until separating one from the other is impossible. And then again, maybe one is the basis for the other. When I first heard the story of the old woman that chases cars away near the area of Sandhill and Sahara, I wondered if this was a real ghost story or urban legend.

Determined to find what I could, my first plan was to discover who this old woman might have been. Then I remembered another "old woman" connected to an earlier investigation. A witness told me, "The ghost is an old woman with red hair, and bright red lipstick. She hangs out in the women's bathroom. Oh yeah, she is wearing high heels."

Hmmm. She must have been very brave to totter about on high heels at such an advanced age, I thought. Then, I asked, "How old would you say she was?"

His reply came fast. "Oh, about 35."

Do I need to tell you that he was maybe 20?

So how old is the ghostly "old gal" near Sandhill and Sahara?

With tape recorder running, and video camera set to catch anything out of the ordinary, a couple of nights were spent just cruising the area. No sign of her! This isn't to say that she doesn't watch the area and shoo cars away. Only that she made no appearance on these two nights. Maybe she is camera shy.

Hmmm! The strip was beckoning, I had this feeling about a certain Megabucks machine…maybe it was ready to make a very wealthy woman of me. Better things to do than wait for some ornery old wraith. Urban legend or ghost?

Urban Legend or Ghost; the Sequel

Is Sandhill a popular spot for specters or what? The flood control tunnels in the area of Sandhill and Charleston are said to resonate with the voices of a young couple who died in a fiery motorcycle crash years ago. It's said that if you listen very closely on the anniversary of their death, you can hear the roar of the motorcycle as it rushes its riders toward their destiny.

What's more, they may not be the only ghosts in residence at this location under the freeway. I talked with someone who said he has heard the sounds of laughter coming from this area late at night. It seems odd the young people who perished in the aforementioned wreck would be laughing. But then again, we aren't ghosts and privy to what they may, or may not, laugh at.

Urban legend or ghosts? It is possible that the unfortunate motorcyclists haunt this area. But the sounds of laughter can probably be attributed to people very much alive....or other ghosts.

Tee for Two

Las Vegans hit the golf courses very early during the summer months. The weather demands it here on the edge of the Mojave Desert. It was barely sun up when Harold got set to tee off at one of the oldest golf courses in town.

"I looked across the green and saw this man walking towards me. What the heck was he doing? I wondered. I yelled for him to get out of the way. But he just stood there looking from side to side, like he was lost or something.

I made to swing my driver and still he didn't budge.

'Hey you! Do you mind moving?' I called to him.

Well, he looks at me like he isn't even seeing me. Then it was like he walked right into nothingness, and was gone. If you're asking what type of clothing he was wearing, or anything like that, I couldn't tell you. No, I don't know what he was, but I can tell you he sure gave me a creepy feeling."

FORE!

Whooooo? Houdini

Houdini never made it to Las Vegas. But that isn't stopping him from being a big draw here. There are special Houdini magic shows, and the collections of Houdini memorabilia, and of course the annual Halloween Houdini séance. Never mind that the magician didn't see fit to heed the call of his beloved wife. Perhaps one day he'll appear at the séance, if only out of curiosity. Don't the living have anything better to do than beckon the dead?

Until then, his fans will have to content themselves with magicians who have mastered some of his escapes. And during those shows, some believe that the spirit of the great Houdini hovers nearby.

Boulder Dam Hotel

Boulder City began as a company town run by the United States Government for the benefit of dam workers and their families. Because of the city's very strict moral code, single workers preferred to spend their leisure and their money in Las Vegas with its gambling, booze and single women.

The only city in Nevada where gambling is not permitted, Boulder City was also the first city in Clark County to have its own airport. During construction of the Hoover Dam, the city was more popular than Las Vegas. Everyone, from the rich and famous, to the just plain curious, flocked to the city just to catch a glimpse of the dam's construction. And they needed a place to stay.

Construction began on the Boulder Dam Hotel in September 1933. Two months later, it was opened with a gala celebration. During its heyday movie stars such as Ronald Coleman, Shirley Temple, Harold Lloyd, Bette Davis and Boris Karloff toured the dam and stayed at the hotel. The reclusive Howard Hughes, who would later change the face of Las Vegas, is rumored to have recuperated at the hotel after the wreck of his private plane on Lake Mead.

Among the spirits thought to haunt this hotel are an elderly gentleman and a young murder victim. Each has been seen throughout the building. One person who visited the hotel recently told of hearing piano music coming from the main floor though no one was playing at the time.

Hoover Dam

He steps from the shadows
with a story to tell.
The dead don't dream,
and they sleep very well.

It was thirteen years from the planning stages to the actual completion of Hoover Dam. During that time 108 men lost their lives working on the project. The ghosts that wander Hoover Dam are thought to be some of these workers or people who have committed suicide at the dam.

Work on the dam was dangerous; several men died by drowning, electrocution, falls and explosions. The Southern Nevada desert heat can be unbearable, especially to those unaccustomed to it. With temperatures soaring well over the one hundred degree mark, work on the dam became even more deadly; thirteen men succumbed to the heat.

Contrary to popular myth, none of those who died while working on Hoover Dam are buried within its concrete walls. Those stories are only the stuff of urban legend. All the bodies of the unfortunate workers that died while working on the dam project were quickly recovered.

However, some of these workers may have chosen to stay on indefinitely. The phantom worker is one spirit that remains on duty at the dam. He is believed to be a young man who died while working the night shift long ago. The ghost usually appears in hard hat and work clothes, ready to put in his time. When he is spotted, it's usually near the elevator and at certain workstations.

The deaths of J.G Tierney and his son Patrick are a strange coincidence connected with the dam. While surveying the location from a boat on the Colorado River, J.G. Tierney fell overboard on December 20, 1922; he was the second man to die on the project. Exactly thirteen years later, to the day, his son Patrick Tierney became the last man to die on the Hoover Dam project when he fell to his death on December 20, 1935.

Hoover Dam is the site of several suicides. This may be due in part to the dam's proximity to Las Vegas. A recent divorcee, saddened with the direction of her life, drove to the dam and jumped into oblivion. When a young couple flew across the country to vacation in Las Vegas, neither of them realized what fate had in store for them. Two days after their arrival, they had a violent argument in their strip hotel room.

He was so enraged that he beat his girlfriend nearly to death, then finished the job by strangling her. When he realized what he'd done, the man sped to Hoover Dam and jumped to his death.

Boulder Theatre   Bill Oberding

Boulder Theatre

New Year's Eve 1934. Las Vegas was not yet the "Entertainment Capital of the World." With the building of Hoover Dam, Boulder City was the spot favored by stars and other tourists. On this night many of Hollywood's top stars were in attendance at the Boulder Theatre for the dazzling world premier of the movie *Silver Streak.*

Movies have not been shown at the theater in many years, yet it remains a place of family entertainment. The dance school that owns the building offers children's dance lessons and seasonal stage productions. As is the case with most theaters, it's said to have its resident ghosts.

Recently a lighting director was working alone in the theater. Engrossed in the task at hand, he happened to look up and see the faint figure of a man slowly walking toward him.

An eerie silence fell on the room as the figure came nearer; the lighting director realized what he was watching was not of this earth.

"Tell you what," he said. "I'll leave you alone if you leave me alone."

As if in agreement the figure vanished.

A tap teacher had a more harrowing experience. As he rehearsed alone one night, he suddenly found himself surrounded by an icy chill.

Curious, he started to look around for the source of the cold breeze, when something, or someone, startled him with a gentle tap on the shoulder.

He is convinced that the theater is haunted. To this day he refuses to be alone in the building after dark. According to some, a man died of a heart attack in the early 1940's while attending a movie at the theater. Some believe this unfortunate man is the source of the haunting.

Boulder City Pet Cemetery

Our pets are treasured companions. They enrich our lives immeasurably, and ask so little in return. Their deaths leave us with empty places in our hearts.

The pet cemetery in Boulder City was started in the early 1950's and continues to grow. Finding the cemetery is not easy. It is not an official cemetery; there are no walls, no iron gates and no expanse of lawn. Yet hundreds of beloved Las Vegas Valley pets lie buried here.

At least one of the cemetery's inhabitants is said to wander this area after dark….

It had only been a week; Sarah was still adjusting to the recent death of her cat. After she got off work at dusk, she drove to the cemetery to visit her pet's grave. As she looked across the site, she thought of her cat as a kitten and how he had scampered about the condominium, so full of life. He was always into mischief. In spite of herself, Sarah smiled at the memory.

In the distance, she noticed a large white cat sauntering toward her.

"Nice kitty." She called absently, her thoughts still on her own cat. At her kind words the cat hurried to her and happily brushed against her legs. Sarah knelt to pet the cat and was stunned when her hand touched nothing but air. She is only one of several people that have seen this ghostly white cat who disappears into thin air.

Clark County Recorder's Office

Those who think Las Vegas is strictly neon and glitz may change their opinion after one look at the Clark County Government Center. Less than a decade old, the building is said to be haunted. Some believe the ghost of an elderly man haunts the Clark County Recorder's Office located on the second floor of the building. Several people who work in the office have seen, or felt his presence. He's also been seen near the rotunda and the stairs.

The ghost is thought to be that of Mr. Clayton, Clark County's first elected recorder. Clayton, so the story goes, met his death one night on the railroad tracks. Misdeed or mishap, no one really knows. The unfortunate man was buried in an unmarked grave and forgotten. Until he started making appearances at the county recorders office. When the new building was completed Clayton's ghost moved in with the recorders office.

Recently a new headstone and grave were donated and Clayton's grave was re-dedicated. Apparently the ghost still makes an occasional appearance at the government center building however.

Fox Ridge Park

As the amount of glass, neon and concrete increases in the city, urban families want to enjoy the outdoors even more. They seek out parks, the places where they can go to barbecue, to picnic, to play and to enjoy nature. With its expanse of lush green lawn, trees and plants, Fox Ridge Park in Henderson is like any other park in the city.

But there is a lonely little ghost who is occasionally seen near the swings here late at night. Many of those who visit this park are unaware of the ghostly little boy and the tragic incident that took place nearby several years ago.

It was the last day of summer. The little boy and his best friend parted company on the corner. They'd spent the day in anticipation of a new school year. There would be a new classroom, and teacher, and the dreaded homework assignments that cut short their playtime. He watched his friend a moment, shrugged and skipped happily toward home. Hamburgers and fries for dinner, his favorite.

As he thought of his meal, danger sped toward him. A drunk driver was behind the wheel of the car that careened around the corner. Before the youngster could react the car slammed into him, killing him instantly.

Since that day the apparition of a little boy has been reportedly seen near the swings. The ghostly child is said to appear after midnight. Some who've seen him say that his face turns into that of a demon if you stare at him, others believe his face is contorted in the agony of knowing how senselessly his life ended.

Moapa Valley High School

Schools, like theaters, top the list of haunted buildings. More often than not, the specters who hang out in these hallowed halls are former students, teachers, or confused children. This isn't the case with the Moapa Valley High School. The school is thought to be haunted by members of the ancient Anasazi civilization.

The Anasazi lived in the Moapa Valley region thousands of years ago. When their culture mysteriously vanished, they left everything behind. Eighty years after the discovery of the Lost City, (Pueblo Grande de Nevada) Anasazi artifacts are occasionally found in this area.

During the construction of the Moapa Valley High School, Anasazi relics were unearthed. Some believe this may even have been an area of ancient burials. Perhaps this is the reason for the unexplained sightings at the school.

Several tall shadowy men have been reported just outside the building. The specters occasionally follow people around the grounds, then vanish as quickly as they appeared. Perhaps these ghostly gents are also responsible for the weeping and singing that reportedly comes from the school late at night also.

Old Logandale School

Located approximately 50 miles southeast of Las Vegas, Logandale is a tiny farming community near Overton and the Lost City Museum. The town is especially proud of its museum and cultural center in the old Logandale School. The school was built in 1935, about the time that Hoover Dam was being completed. The first school in Nevada to implement a hot lunch program for its students, the Logandale School charged only ten cents for the meal. Children whose families could not afford the dime were fed anyway.

When a new school was built, the community found other uses for the old school including funeral parlor and meeting place. The ghost that usually grabs attention is that of a sandy haired little boy who is believed to have died near the school long ago. He is mischievous and doesn't mind tapping someone on the shoulder, or turning on the water faucets in the women's bathroom.

The ghostly little boy may not be the only revenant in residence. At least one person who works in the building believes that a former librarian stays around to make sure that everything is in order at the old school. Whenever anything is misplaced, she is called upon to help locate it. Invariably, the missing item turns up.

Pioneer Saloon   Bill Oberding

Pioneer Saloon

Goodsprings is about 40 miles southwest of Las Vegas. This tiny town of approximately 200 is a world apart. There is no neon, traffic jams or overcrowding here. In 1914 this area was rich in zinc and copper. World War I caused the prices of these metals to skyrocket. This brought an influx of money, businesses and people to Goodsprings. At one time there were more than thirty mines operating in the area.

These days the town is relatively quiet. There is no sign of the mining activity that once took place here. Over in the old cemetery a couple of ghostly children are said to roam at nights. Ghosthunting groups have done several investigations there, but the two little specters have not been positively identified. Who they were remains a mystery. A favorite with ghosthunters happens to be the locals' hangout as well, the Pioneer Saloon where friendly barkeeps and old west style décor lend a certain aura of down home fun. Built in 1913, the Pioneer Saloon is haunted by the ghost of a card playing gambler whose cheating ways spelled his doom.

Shot dead at the poker table, the bewhiskered gambler is said to roam the premises still. Some have seen his apparition standing at the front door or sitting at the end of the bar. Bullet holes in the tin building are thought to be remnants of that shooting,

He is not the only ghost at the saloon. The spirit of movie star Carole Lombard, some say, also haunts this building. A wall in the poolroom honors both Lombard and her husband Clark Gable. Ms. Lombard was killed in 1942 when her plane slammed into nearby Mount Potosi. Clark

Gable spent those anxious hours awaiting word of survivors at the El Rancho Vegas in Las Vegas and the Fayle Hotel and Pioneer Saloon here in Goodsprings.

For many years afterwards, according to some long time Las Vegans, pieces of the wreckage were visible whenever the sunlight reflected off of them.

Mount Potosi Bureau of Land Management Nevada Field Office

A Star Dies on Mt. Potosi

Besides Lombard, twenty-one others were aboard the TWA plane when it crashed enroute from Las Vegas to Los Angeles. Lombard, who had done her part for the war effort was returning from a successful campaign of selling war bonds.

The crash location on the side of Double Mountain (Mount Potosi) and the weather hampered the rescue effort. It was mid January; snow was already heavy in the high mountain regions. From a makeshift operations headquarters in Goodsprings, searchers hiked up the side of the mountain toward the crash site. Theirs, they soon discovered, was not to be a rescue mission.

Charred and broken bodies were strewn around the wreckage. One person would later say that the snow was red with blood. Ms. Lombard's burned body was discovered under one of the wings. But it would take dental charts flown in from Hollywood, to positively identify the blonde comedian.

As the bodies were recovered, they were wrapped in brown army blankets, carefully hoisted down the cliff and taken by horse to Goodsprings. Army ambulances transported them on to Las Vegas.

By all accounts Carole Lombard loved to party and have a good time....Does she haunt the Pioneer Saloon? That depends on who you ask.

Las Vegas circa 1930-1940   Author's collection

Landmark Hotel circa 1970 Author's collection

CASINOS

Where the fun never sets....Sands Hotel slogan

Luxor Sphinx   Peggy Oberding

Luxor

This is a town steeped in superstition. How could it be otherwise? Everyday thousands of gamblers come to bet the odds, or against them, in casinos large and small. Helping to keep the casinos running smoothly are the thousands of men and women whose jobs are to see that the customer is always happy and satisfied.

Some toss cards, serve drinks, refill the empty hoppers of slot machines, mix drinks, collect Keno tickets, serve meals, sweep floors, ensure the safety of the casino's patrons, and the list of jobs goes on and on. Many are as superstitious as the patrons they serve. It's okay; it's to be expected. Step on a crack and break your mother's back…………….

Like a sentinel guarding its city, the sphinx faces eastward toward the rising sun. Passengers on arriving and departing planes are given a glimpse of the majestic creature. Many are unaware that the glaring bright light atop the pyramid was visible to astronauts whose capsules encircled the earth. Most of them probably don't know that some in Las Vegas believe the light should be capped in order to bring good luck to the city.

The Luxor is not without its ghosts. A workman fell to his death during the construction of the Luxor; he is said to haunt the building still. Then there is the story of the out of town businessman down on his luck and lonely; suicide seemed like a way out. Unfortunately it wasn't. Some claim to have seen the apparition of the middle-aged man as he wanders aimlessly through the upper hallways.

One person told of seeing a man in a brown suit approaching her in the hall. As they came face to face, instead of sidestepping, the man walked right through her. As he did so she felt an icy shiver.

A young man decided to end it all by jumping from the 8th floor to the casino floor below. As he fell, he yelled triumphantly. Luckily no one else was injured when he landed near the hotel reservation desk.

Saddest of all is the ghostly young woman who has reportedly seen in the casino area. Shortly after the Luxor's opening, the distraught young woman walked into the building and purposely strode to the elevator. She got off on one of the top floors; there she stood in the hall watching the casino action far below. Anyone who saw her at that moment might have thought she was just another tourist fascinated by the Luxor's unique structure.

And then, without warning, she climbed up on the railing.....leapt off...and came crashing down onto the casino.

The Plaza

The Plaza is located across the street from the light show extravaganza, known as the Fremont Experience. The high rise hotel/casino is in the heart of old downtown Las Vegas, near the site of the old train station. There may be a few spirits of those who met death on the railroad tracks lurking about, but the most talked about ghostly inhabitant here is said to be a stagehand who hanged himself on an empty stage decades ago.

Apparently the man was distraught over a love affair gone sour and saw no other way to stop the pain. It's been said that suicide is a permanent solution to a temporary problem. It certainly wasn't the answer to this young man's troubles.

He's rumored to still be on the premises; now it seems he might regret his hasty decision to end it all. This prankster likes the showroom, but he is usually in the dressing rooms; as might be expected, the focus of his ghostly antics is the beautiful showgirls who perform here. He has been known to tap showgirls on the shoulder, blow icy air in their ears, and move their makeup.

Sahara Hotel/Casino

A slight breeze sent an early morning winter chill cutting across the valley. The sun was just starting to sparkle over Sunrise Mountain as early risers began casino hopping for the best breakfast deals. All you can eat and a roll of nickels, such a deal!

Breakfast and the chance to win a jackpot at one of the slots meant nothing to him. He had come here for one reason. Security guards were suspicious of him the moment they spotted him on the 23rd floor. Trained to know the look, they questioned him and sent him on his way. An hour later he came scurrying back.

This time they issued sterner warnings. He wasn't a hotel guest; they'd asked him to leave. Now he was for all intents and purposes, a trespasser. Trespassers could be arrested. No, he didn't want to spend time in the Clark County Jail. He slinked away. But he was determined. He went back up to the 23rd floor and stood on the ledge for a moment before jumping. Two tourists out for an early morning breakfast special, witnessed him come crashing to the street. Suddenly they weren't so hungry after all.

Haunted Hotel Room

Several people have told similar stories concerning this particular ghost sighting at one of Las Vegas' most fabulous hotel/casinos.

Mark and Leslie Jones arrived in Las Vegas from a small town in the northwest expecting to be awed. They were that and more.

Typical first time tourists, they gawked all the way from McCarran International to the hotel. Neither of them had ever seen anything that even came close to Las Vegas...especially at night! The sun had long ago set, but the temperature was still hovering at 100 degrees; when they stepped out of the airport limo, the desert heat was like a slap in the face to the two coastal dwellers.

After a quick shower, they hit the casino floor and stayed at the Blackjack tables for several hours. It was nearing midnight when they decided to grab a couple of sandwiches and head for their room. Leslie left Mark to get their food and went upstairs. Exhausted, she stretched out on the king size bed and quickly fell asleep. A moment later she was startled awake by a man's voice asking, "Who are you?"

She sat bolt upright and stared in disbelief as the image of a man drifted across the room. He seemed to almost

167

glow, and instinctively she realized he was not of this world. Oddly enough, she wasn't frightened.

There was something about his sad, perplexed expression that evoked pity; she stared at him until she heard Mark opening the door.

"What is that?" he asked nodding toward the man.

Leslie shrugged, "It's a ghost."

No sooner were the words out of her mouth than the apparition quickly dissolved.

As they hungrily ate their sandwiches they discussed the ghostly man and finally decided that he meant them no harm. The next day they rented a car and drove to the Valley of Fire. After a day of exploring they headed for the Blackjack tables; by the time they were crawling into bed, they had forgotten all about the ghost. They might have continued to do so had he not appeared to them that night.

Mark wasn't the least bit interested in who the ghost was or why he was in the room. But Leslie was determined to find out what she could about him; it was obvious he had been in some kind of distress. After breakfast she started asking hotel personnel about the ghost; no one knew a thing. Most of them looked at her as if she was crazy to even ask.

But Leslie didn't give up so easily. While Mark played the slots, she took a cab to the library and started looking in the old newspaper files. Two hours later, she'd found what she was looking for. The face of the man who'd been in the hotel room smiled at her from the screen of the microfiche machine. The story told of how he'd been the victim of a robbery murder in the stairwell of the hotel/casino.

Saddened by the man's story, she decided to help him by explaining that he was dead and telling him to go toward the light. She didn't get the chance. He did not appear in the room again during their stay.

The Mirage

Is there a ghost in one of the Mirage's bathrooms? Some say there is. Singer, Comedian/Impressionist Danny Gans is one of Las Vegas' top entertainers. For several years in a row he's been voted the city's "Entertainer of the Year." His shows are always sold-out successes, and as might be expected tickets are in high demand. Gans performs in the Mirage Hotel Casino at the fabulous 1,250 seat theater that bears his name.

The bathrooms nearby are rumored to be the domain of a prankster ghost that takes delight in playing with the automatic sensor faucets. Maybe it's a ghost…maybe the sensors simply malfunction on occasion. It is a curious fact that bathrooms are so often said to be haunted.

Stratosphere

Many Las Vegans, especially the new ones, use the Stratosphere as the guidepost that helps them find their way around the city, and prevents them from getting lost. The Stratosphere can be seen from any location in Las Vegas. No wonder! It is the tallest structure west of the Mississippi. Of course there is the casino/hotel, and in addition to a revolving restaurant, gift shops, and a rollercoaster, the outdoor observation deck features a view of the Las Vegas area that is not to be missed. According to some a ghostly man is often seen in the casino area near the elevators. This young man has been known to simply vanish before people's eyes.

An area outside the hotel/casino is also thought to be haunted. During the early morning hours soft whispering can sometimes be heard. The discussion of resident ghosts is generally not encouraged by hotel/casinos, especially those of suicides. However, some employees insist that the ghost is that of a young man who leapt to his death from the top of the observation deck. Some of those that remember the incident say that when he was told to be careful, the man turned and calmly waved to the security guards; then dove headfirst from the tower.

The closer one is to the Stratosphere Tower, the harder this is to imagine.

Many paranormal researches cite suicide as a primary reason for a haunting to occur. Apparently the taking of one's own life does not solve problems; a ghost may stay indefinitely trying to sort out what went wrong.

The Flamingo circa 1950   Author's collection

The Flamingo Hotel

There have been numerous sightings of Bugsy Siegel at the Flamingo Hotel. The ghostly gangster prefers the Flamingo even thought nothing remains of the Flamingo that he built back in 1946 except for a plaque in the rose garden.

Complete with swans, waterfalls, birds, roses and brightly colored Koi fish, the Flamingo Hotel's rose garden is a great way to spend an afternoon in Vegas.

Bugsy's smiling phantom has been spotted in different areas of the Flamingo several times. Always the sharp dresser, the ghostly gangster is nattily attired in a smoking jacket and slacks of the forties style. He seems to prefer the rose garden and the wedding chapel area.

One person, who saw the ghostly Bugsy recalls, "I'll never forget that day. It was raining and everyone was running for cover. I happened to look at the plaque marker. That's when I saw him. He looked real and yet he didn't. His clothes were out of style. Like something you might see in one of those old Humphrey Bogart movies. Then it dawned on me.

Am I seeing a ghost? I walked a little closer to get a better look. It looked like he was talking, but no words were coming out. It was Bugsy Siegel all right. I've seen enough pictures of him to know.

I was soaking wet. And scared. I turned to see if anyone else was seeing what I was. When I turned back to look at him, he was gone. There's no way a real person could have done that."

Before it was demolished in the late 90's Bugsy's former penthouse was a favorite with tourists. It was also the place of numerous "Bugsy sightings."

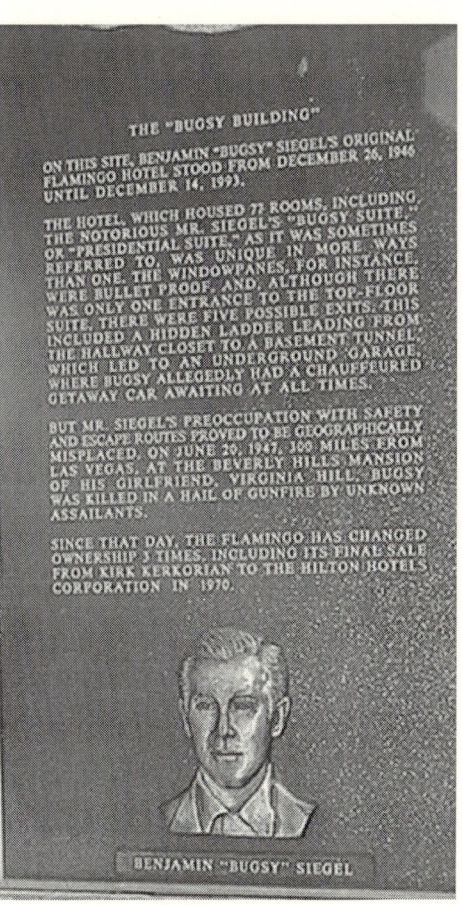

Close up of Bugsy's plaque

Napkin from the Flamingo

Bugsy Siegel Commemorative chip   Jonell Johnson

Keno...Can You?

Anyone who has ever ran Keno for a living knows it's a tough job. Hot footing it through a crowded casino coffee shop and trying to pick up Keno tickets, while talking with customers who are in various stages of devouring their meals...it ain't easy. The same lame jokes. Keno, did you lose your little dog? I bet you go dancing when you get off shift!

Yeah and I bet you have some manners when you're back home in Hayseed or Bumpkin Town or wherever the Hell you came from.

Like Las Vegas and the rest of the world, the Keno game has changed. If it hasn't been abandoned altogether, the game is downsized to the point it is little more than a cubbyhole in an out of the way corner in most casinos. Gone are the days when there was a distinction between a runner's job and that of a writer. Runners ran Keno tickets and writers wrote them. Efficiency and the bottom line require writers run and runners write. Thus the distinctions are blurred to oblivion.

Once writing Keno tickets was an art form, writers prided themselves on the beauty of their spots and the speed in which they slapped them on a ticket. Ink spatters on otherwise white cuffs were badges of honor. And 56 way 9's were impressive tickets that demanded skill and knowledge to figure out. Eight groups of three, a 56 way 9, could break the heart and boggle the mind, of any break-in* that dared to figure one out for the first time. Computers were introduced into the game a couple of decades ago, and the Keno game was changed forever.

Gone are the spinning cages, inkpots, and brushes, the Bates machines, the punch machines, and the need to change the paper after every game. No one knows how to figure tickets anymore. Why should they? The computer has all the pays on every ticket in the game figured within seconds after the last ball is in the tube.

In the early days, Keno runners ran through the casino on feet that sometimes ached, racking up mile after mile in an eight hour shift. The longer they were in the game, the more appealing the sit down job of the writer became.

No one wanted to make a career of running Keno. The work was too grueling for the money one was paid. Those runners not headed to cocktails or the pit aspired to be writers. Just as soon as they could wield the brush correctly. Just as soon as they could make spots that looked like sails. Just as soon as they could figure out a 66 way 6 or any other ticket their training writer tossed their way.

Now it's the slots that are hot! The pit is a draw…And Keno…well some refer to it as a dying game…while the game offers the worst odds to player, it is not a big money maker for the house. Many players consider the game too complicated, others say it is too slow. This, the computer, and the Keno slot machines are surely the death knell for the Keno game. Did a Keno game really help to finance the Great Wall of China?

If it says so in the payout book its gotta be true!

In the early 1970's the Keno game was still going strong...And it was one of the easiest ways for future Blackjack dealers, and cocktail waitresses to get their feet in the door. A former head of personnel once joked that nearly every new hire did a stint in Keno first. "This way," he laughed, "they will appreciate their jobs more."

In the fall of 1975 Avery Wilson was at last 21 years old. One of the first things she did as a legal adult, besides play the slots, was give her notice at the fast food restaurant where she worked. Then she applied for a job as a Keno runner. A few days later she was on the floor and in training. Stamina, patience, a good personality, and an excellent memory, she had them all, and soon she was on her way to being a top Keno runner.

No one in Keno figured Avery long for the game. She was just too pretty not to have caught the eyes of the pit bosses and the bar managers. One or the other was sure to ask that she be transferred to his department. Besides her good looks, the young woman was bubbly, enthusiast and kind; everybody, who knew her, liked her. She would be missed when that transfer finally came.

It never did. One night after work, Avery stopped at the convenience store near her home and walked in on a robbery. Startled, the robber shot and killed the store clerk then turned the gun on Avery. The Keno department was stunned. Death shouldn't happen to someone so young and vibrant and so full of life...But life isn't always fair. The young woman they all liked was gone.

But was she? The first person to see her was another Keno runner who swore she'd seen her in the restroom. And then a writer on the graveyard shift saw her at the Keno counter, someone else saw her in the restaurant and in the pit. Years passed, the city grew, the old had to make way for the new. Eventually the casino was demolished; hopefully the young Keno runner has moved on.

* a break-in is a trainee.

MGM Grand Fire

Ballys is a magnificent hotel/casino that stands where the original MGM Grand once stood. For this reason, some believe that Ballys is haunted by a terrible tragedy that took place here decades ago. Others insist that the stories of ghostly weeping and of apparitions who appear to be disoriented, are nothing but the products of overworked imaginations.

Living on the edge of the Mojave Desert makes Las Vegans especially sensitive to the cold. On November 20, 1980 the temperature dipped; it might have seemed chilly to those who called Las Vegas home. But it was toasty warm to the thousands of out of towners who crammed into the city all set to gamble, golf, and soak up some sunshine.

Comdek, the electronic convention was in town, as a result business was brisk everywhere. The MGM Grand was at 99% capacity. Built in 1973, the towering twenty-six stories tall MGM Grand was one of the newest and most elegant hotel/casinos in Las Vegas, a new standard. Many of the hotel's guests had come from faraway places where snow was already piled high. But this was Las Vegas, a mecca for those fleeing the biting cold of other climes.

Some of the guests spent part of that last carefree night, at Mac Davis' show in the 900 seat Celebrity Room; others parked happily at slot machines, and some played Blackjack under dazzling chandeliers in the pit. None of them could have known what horror waited; tragedy and death would claim some of them. No one who stayed at the MGM Grand this night would come away unscathed.

Early on the morning of November 21th 1980 many Las Vegans were still fast asleep. When they awoke, it would be to the news of the fire and the horror at the MGM Grand Hotel. The fire started in the kitchen and rushed through the casino floor killing all in its wake. Some of those trapped in the upper floors leapt to their deaths rather than die in the flames. By the time the fire was contained it had become one of the worst hotel fires in the world; the death toll was 87.

The fire-damaged building was repaired; new fire safety codes were enacted as a result of the tragic MGM Grand fire. The hotel was re-opened and it was business as usual.

Pitching Cards and Seeing Phantoms

Dealers. Blackjack dealers, twenty-one dealers. Their job is to stand in the pit and pitch cards to casino patrons. Seems easy enough; It's not! Dealing cards requires concentration, and personality and a thick skin; this is especially true when an irate customer resorts to verbal insults after losing hand after hand, or a pit boss starts sweating another customer's big winning streak. Either way, the dealer generally bears the brunt of the anger.

Unflinching concentration, no doubt this is why Blackjack dealers are accorded regular 20-minute breaks throughout their shifts. Forty minutes on, twenty minutes off, just enough time to grab a sandwich, a smoke or visit with fellow dealers. Generally considered the elite in casino hierarchy, dealers customarily sit with each other.

One Saturday night the dealers had plenty to talk about. Within an hour of one another two tourists toppled off their high-backed chairs, dead before they hit the carpet was the general consensus. No one likes to talk about customers who die in the casinos, it's bad for business. And what's bad for business is just plain bad. The paramedics rushed in and whisked the unfortunate men out ASAP.

Gone and forgotten. Then Rusty, a redhead who had dealt cards at the establishment for more years than she cared to think about, saw one of the men standing right there at her table. Looking forlorn and confused, the specter turned and vanished as quickly as he'd appeared. She knew what she'd seen, but was wise enough to keep it to herself. Within a week of her sighting, Rusty overheard another dealer talking about seeing the ghost walk through the pit. She kept silent, but the others continued to talk.

Pit bosses hear it all; what they don't hear they see. Like other members of casino management, they are sometimes referred to as "the suits." And like other members of management, the pit boss keeps an eye and an ear on the casino's best interests. Before long the whispers made their way to the ears of Rusty's pit boss, and he was furious.

What if customers heard the story? It could dampen the enthusiasm of especially superstitious players. Then too, they might go elsewhere to gamble, God forbid! Think of the bottom line. The hush was on.. No more talk of a ghost in the pit. Occasionally Rusty would see the ghostly gent standing at her table, but thankfully he never pulled up a chair and placed a bet.

Ghostly Showgirl

Men may fantasize about them, women might envy them, but their work is grueling and their careers are short lived. Even in the hands of the most skilled plastic surgeon, no one can hang on to beauty and youth forever. Gravity takes its toll and endurance fades; who really wants to strut across a stage wearing a scattering of sequins, a hot pink feathered headdress and little else at age fifty?

When a showgirl had the misfortune of being murdered in her apartment no one realized that she might decide to stick around for a while. Apparently she did.

Margo was a Blackjack dealer on the graveyard shift. Until she moved into an older apartment complex her thoughts on ghostly activity were ambivalent. It didn't take long for her to discover that she was sharing her home with a ghost.

Almost from the day she moved in, Margo had an unshakeable feeling that she was not really alone in the little four-room unit. She'd heard the stories about a showgirl being strangled in the apartment. That had happened in the 1960's; she doubted it would have any affect on her life.

Her hairbrush and makeup were often misplaced, and she found her books and magazines in the oddest places. She assured herself it was merely forgetfulness. When her perfume started to smell like an entirely different fragrance, she blamed it on her allergies.

One morning halfway through her shift, Margo suddenly became so ill she had to take an eo* .

"I was so sick it's a wonder I was able to drive home. When I got there, I practically crawled into my apartment and barely had the strength to throw myself on the sofa. I lay on the sofa a little while and then I heard what sounded like humming in the bedroom. My first thought was that I'd left the radio on. I listened for a few minutes and went in to turn it off.

That's when I saw her sitting at the foot of the bed; she stared into the mirror and applied lipstick. A feeling of sadness rushed over me...She was nearly transparent and seemed to be glowing; I knew she wasn't real. Telling myself that she must be the showgirl who was murdered in the apartment, I summoned up my courage and spoke softly.

'I know it was a terrible thing that happened to you. But that was a long time ago and you can't stay here any longer. You don't belong here anymore. It's time for you to move on.'

She turned, smiled at me and quickly vanished....It's weird. I never saw or heard her again. And nothing was ever again misplaced

Whiskey Pete's

Whiskey Pete's is located in Primm, on the California/Nevada border some 35 miles west of Las Vegas. The casino was built on land once owned by a cantankerous old curmudgeon who supplemented his income by selling bootleg whiskey. His gas station was the last place to fill up before heading out into the Mojave Desert. That fact and his whiskey made for a popular stopping place.

When he died, they buried him on his property. And there, so the story goes, he rested for decades. Until progress came calling. The area where he slumbered eternally was needed for other purposes. And so Whiskey Pete remains were moved to another location. This hasn't stopped him from enjoying the casino activities. The ghostly old Pete has been seen throughout the casino, watching gamblers intently. If only he'd thought of this!

Ponderin' the Purple Haze at the Trop

The Trop as locals refer to it, has been part of Las Vegas history for decades. Known as the "Tiffany of the Strip," the Tropicana features Les Folies Bergere, the oldest show of its kind in Las Vegas; think feathers, and sequins and gorgeous women cavorting across the stage topless.

Nothing unusual about that. This is Las Vegas, after all.

The only thing unusual here is the mysterious purple haze that some say hovers at the front of the Trop. This haze supposedly shows up in photos on occasion. What? A camera monopolizing purple haze? Hoping for a glimpse, I recently took several pics. Not once did the haze appear. Hmmm. Cold be this haze is the ghost of a long ago employee, or a light refraction.

Epilogue...

Las Vegas is not the dark foreboding place of film noir. Neither is it the bright and always-a-happy-ending city. To assume either would be naïve.

Certainly no one can deny that the city is unique. There are thousands of reasons for this. Being haunted is not one of them. Ghosts and hauntings phenomena occur throughout the world.

No, what sets this city apart is its quirkiness to the core, and the eccentricities of those spirits who take the *"What happens in Las Vegas, stays in Las Vegas"* slogan seriously.

Las Vegas, you gotta love it!

Bibliography

Books

Ashbaugh, Don *Nevada's Turbulent Yesterday* Westernlore Press 1963

Castleman, Deke *Las Vegas* Compass American Guides Oakland Calif. 1991

Coakley, Deirdre with Greenspun, Hank, Gerard, Gary C. and the staff of the Las Vegas Sun...*The Day the MGM Grand Hotel Burned* Lyle Stuart Inc, Secaucus, N.J. 1982

Denton, Sally and Morris, Roger *The Money and the Power The Making of Las Vegas And Its Hold on America 1947-2000* Alfred A. Knopf New York 2001

Eisenberg, Dennis Dan, Uri Landau, Eli *Meyer Lansky Mogul of the Mob* Paddingon Press LTD New York and London 1979

Jennings, Dean *We Only Kill Each Other* Pocket Books 1992

Johnston, David *Temples of Chance How America Inc. Bought Out Murder Inc. to Win Control of the Casino Business* Doubleday New York, New York 1992

Land, Barbara and Land, Myrick *A Short History of Las Vegas* University of Nevada Press Reno Las Vegas 1999

Levy, Shaun *Rat Pack Confidential*

McBride, Dennis *Midnight on Arizona Street: The Secret Life of the Boulder Dam Hotel* Boulder City/Hoover Dam Museum 1993

McCracken, Robert D. *Las Vegas The Great American Playground* University of Nevada Press Reno 1996

Moehring, Eugene P. *Resort City in the Sunbelt Las Vegas, 1930-1970* University of Nevada Press Reno Nevada 1989

Newton, Wayne *Once Before I Go* William Morrow and Company Inc. New York, New York 1989

Oberding, Janice *Haunted Nevada 2nd Edition* Thunder Mountain Productions Press Reno, Nevada 2004

Paher, Stanley W. *Las Vegas As it began as it grew* Nevada Publications Las Vegas Nevada 1971

Patera, Alan H. *Goodsprings Nevada* Western Places 1999

Reid, Ed and Demaris, Ovid *The Green Felt Jungle* Pocketbooks New York 1964

Roemer, William F. Jr. *The Enforcer Spilotro The Chicago Mob's Man Over Las Vegas* Donald I. Fine Inc. New York 1994

Roske, Ralph J. *Las Vegas A Desert Paradise* Continental Heritage Press Inc. Tulsa Oklahoma 1986

Rothman, Hal *Neon Metropolis* Routledge New York NY. 2002

Scott, Cathy *The Killing of Tupac Shakur* Huntington Press Las Vegas Nevada 1997

Spanier, David *Welcome to the Pleasuredome Inside Las Vegas....* London 1992

Stevens, Joseph E. *Hoover Dam An American Adventure* University of Oklahoma Press Norman and London 1988

Thomas, Bob *Liberace* St. Martin's Press New York 1987

Wilkerson, William III *The Man Who Invented Las Vegas*

Periodicals

Bond, Tiffannie *Mr. Petrie Spooks School* Southeast View October 25, 2000

Mikkelsen, Ginger *Ghost Stories; Clark County Employees Share Ghost Stories* Southeast View January 2, 2002

Index

About the Author

Janice Oberding worked in management within the gaming industry for many years. She is the author of numerous books on Nevada's history and paranormal. Her books include Haunted Nevada, Ghosthunters' Guide to Virginia City, Haunted Gold and Silver and Legends and Ghosts of the Lake Tahoe Area.

In addition to teaching classes on ghosthunting, and online writing, she has acted as a technical advisor for many television shows, and has guest starred in episodes of the Scariest Places on Earth, Haunted Travels and Dead Famous.
http://www.hauntednevada.com

Thunder Mountain Productions Press
PO Box 19514
Reno, Nevada 89511

Printed in the United States